STORIES FROM SOMEWHERE IN THE SKIES

RYAN SPRAGUE

Foreword by
DR. D.W. PASKULA

BEYOND THE FRAY
Publishing

ISBN 13: 978-1-954528-68-0

Cover Art by: **Caitlyn Grabenstein - @cult.class**

Beyond The Fray Publishing, a division of Beyond The Fray, LLC, San Diego, CA
www.beyondthefraypublishing.com

BEYOND THE FRAY
Publishing

CONTENTS

Special thanks to all those who submitted their stories in the past and in the future.

Your courage, honesty, and willingness to share these extraordinary moments of your life truly helps drive this conversation forward.

This book is for you.

"Seeing is believing. But feeling is truth."

– Thomas Fuller, 17th Century Clergyman

FOREWORD

The bravest among us support those whose stories often go untold, and within these pages, Ryan Sprague shows that he is not afraid to stand by the witnesses to humanity's greatest mystery—UFO phenomena. Yet for more than seventy years in the United States these stories were untold. Programs of disinformation, including the stigmatization of witnesses, created a climate of fear and reticence in the reporting of these mysterious aerial objects. In *Stories from Somewhere in the Skies*, Sprague focuses on his *Witness Accounts*, the oral records of accounts by everyday people and military personnel who've seen extraordinary aerial phenomena. Here they have been transcribed into a written record.

The effort to document important stories and oral traditions is among the most important endeavors in a world where exponential change has only just begun. Sprague's efforts parallel those of anthropologists who document the oral traditions of disappearing indigenous cultures, and scientists who urgently record the songs of whales and other species whose future existence are not assured. Not only will these accounts sustain the continuity of the historical record, but they are fascinating, absorbing tales of mystery and wonder.

Sprague interviews a variety of people, all of whom have in common that they never sought to see a UFO. This sets Sprague's work apart from almost all other media about the topic. He covers the stories and experiences of people who haven't been chosen, those who did not want to be pilots or aerospace scientists, but nevertheless have confronted the ineffable and are coming to terms with what that means for them, and for us.

Sprague's work is based on the lived reality of the phenomena and not on the media narratives that circulate about it. I've made this comparison before: In this sense, Sprague's work embodies the strategy of one of the best researchers of the phenomena: Dr. Jacques Vallee. Vallee cautioned researchers to stay away from the media frenzy around UFO events, and instead focus on the local, the personal, and those cases that were not the focus of media, Hollywood, or Netflix. Sprague's work is authentic in important ways, as he interviews ordinary people who have been changed in ways that reorient their values and lives. As they open their minds to the realities of the cosmos, they do not take life for granted. Sprague's work opens this world to us, in accessible and refreshingly non-politicized language. It is clear that as we gather more data about the phenomena, our understanding of it will evolve, and this is especially true when we listen to the voices of those who experience it. And Sprague has always been and continues to be at the center of this rapidly changing story, to dissect it and make sense of these stories, one experience at a time.

Dr. Diana Walsh Pasulka
University of North Carolina, Wilmington

INTRODUCTION

It had been twenty-seven years since I last stood on that dock. But there I was, listening to nothing but the sound of water splashing the underside of the rotted wood planks beneath my feet. It was the only thing left of the Fisherman's Wharf, a small little motel tucked snugly on the edge of the Saint Lawrence River in Alexandria Bay, New York. The dock was nothing more than a relic now, the motel itself being replaced by a modest summer home.

It was August of 2022, and almost to the day, I had finally made it back to the exact location where my life had fundamentally changed. Where I had stared up into the night skies and had something truly extraordinary stare back. The memories began to flood in with the sound of splashing water below.

It was the summer of 1995. The sun had set, the clear night sky bringing with it a landscape of endless stars. I was alone on the dock, fishing. My mother, father, and sister were inside our motel room, relaxing, while I savored the final moments of sunlight over this long and winding body of water situated between central New York and Ontario, Canada. I was twelve years old at the time, reveling in the solitude that often plagued many soon-to-be teenagers. And also, like many teenagers in the mid '90s, I was listening to Green Day on my portable CD player. At the moment, "Basket Case," the seventh track on the album, was blasting through my headphones as I reeled my fishing line in. I looked down to see if my bait was still on the hook, when I noticed something odd in the water. A light.

I pulled the line up and set my pole on the dock, crouching down to look into the water. I suddenly noticed two other lights below the original.

The closer I got to the surface of the water, the sooner I realized these lights weren't in the shallow depths, but were reflections from above. That's when my attention moved to the darkening skies, and my heart immediately dropped. I ripped the headphones from my ears and dropped the portable CD player on the dock. I stared upward at what I could only perceive as a perfect equilateral triangle formation of lights. What struck me was that these were much larger than the stars around the formation, and I could see no stars between the space the triangle formation took up, giving the impression that whatever this was, it was solid. And big. And close.

I continued staring up at this formation, noticing two other distinctions in that moment. There seemed to be some sort of hazy, reddish-orange light towards the center of the formation. It was different from the white lights on each point, as this center light was almost pulsating. The second distinction was that, while even at age twelve I knew airplanes made sound, this aerial "thing" was completely silent. All I heard was the sound of the water splashing on the underside of the dock. I continued watching this silent display above me as the formation began to glide over the water and head towards the other side of the river. I was both scared, but also in awe. I felt frozen and as if I were somehow glued to the dock.

I had to put this moment into some semblance of reality. I had to know I wasn't imagining this. And if I wasn't, I had to know that whatever it was, it could be explained. I was able to finally yell for my family to come out of the motel room. My father, closest to the door, ran outside, thinking I'd perhaps fallen into the water. He was relieved to see I hadn't. However, it was clear to him that I was staring at something in the sky. He stood beside me on the dock and looked up. That was when I truly knew I wasn't imagining any of this. Something was up there, and we were both watching it as it continued to glide away into the distance.

I stood there, my eyes moving to my father's face, waiting for some sort of reaction. Or more importantly, an explanation. Neither came. He continued watching as this silent triangle of lights soon disappeared into the dark void of the night. A small, quizzical impression overtook my father's face for a brief moment. He shrugged and gave me a simple, "Huh..."

I watched my father walk off the dock and back in the motel. There was a Yankees game on television, and even this strange experience wasn't going to tear him away from that for too long. I stood there for what felt like hours, still trying to process what had happened. It was a mere fifty feet or so to the door of our motel room, and as I made my way there, I turned to look over my shoulder out at the water and sky, both hoping and dreading the sight of the triangle again. Luckily, it never returned that night.

We left the motel the following morning. However, that triangular formation would return in my dreams for many years to come, leaving me hungry for answers, but also afraid of those answers if I ever got them. It's a fear I sometimes feel today as I continue to struggle with what happened on the dock that night.

Here I was, twenty-seven years later, standing on the dock, and still no closer to those answers. But the journey between 1995 and 2022 had not only been profound, but life-changing. While life certainly went on for me in every way, this UFO sighting inspired an entire shift in what I chose to do with that life: travel the world finding others who'd seen UFOs and advocating for a widespread public acceptance of the UFO topic. But perhaps most importantly: seeking both answers and closure, both for myself and the thousands of individuals all over the world who have seen something in the skies they can't explain.

These sightings and experiences afford a large spectrum of implication for the observers and experiencers. I wanted to both preserve these stories for those who had the courage to tell them, and also provide an outlet to share this part of their lives that many kept hidden. Until now.

The *Somewhere in the Skies* podcast is a pseudo-epilogue to my book *Somewhere in the Skies: A Human Approach to the UFO Phenomenon*. An epilogue that continues to be written as the podcast grows and as more individuals continue to reach out to me to tell their UFO stories. Within the scope of the podcast, I created a series titled *Witness Accounts*. Each episode of this series features a handful of witnesses submitting their stories, in their own words, without interruption, and at their own pace. My only request for these submissions was to detail the sighting or experience the best they can, and to describe if and how it impacted them. I was completely overwhelmed with the magnitude and the intimacy with which complete strangers would share their personal stories, knowing that thousands of people would hear it. It continues to be a commendable contribution to not only the podcast, but to the entire UFO research community who strive for legitimacy. With the *Witness Accounts* series, my true goal is to show the public that every day people in all walks of life have had UFO sightings and encounters. People just like you and me. The stories you'll read in the upcoming pages of this book come directly from the words of those who experienced them. These are, by far, some of the most powerful and profound accounts in the *Somewhere in the Skies* archives.

A lot has happened in the past few years when it comes to UFOs. In 2017, an article in the *New York Times* exposed a once-secretly-run investigation within the Pentagon, known as the Advanced Aerospace Threat Identification Program (AATIP). In the archives of the *Somewhere in the Skies* podcast, you'll hear several interviews with former US Army Counterintelligence special agent and former employee of the Office of the Under Secretary of Defense for Intelligence Luiz Elizondo, who ran the program. Within this endeavor were dozens of documented reports of UFOs being sighted in or around sensitive military operations and training areas. This included the now famous 2004 *Nimitz* UFO incident where a Tic Tac-shaped object was intercepted by US Navy fighter pilots. Alleged video of this object was officially released by the Department of Defense in April of 2020.

In my 2020 book, you'll find an entire chapter dedicated to Chief Radar Operator Kevin Day, who was the first to track the Tic Tac object and order jets to be scrambled to investigate. The event itself had a major negative impact on Day's life after it happened. It wasn't until other service members went public with their involvement that Day finally found vindication and solace in the dramatic event that had unfolded. You'll also find interviews in the archives of the *Somewhere in the Skies* podcast with various other witnesses to the 2004 *Nimitz* event, including former US naval aviator Lieutenant Commander Alex Dietrich, who intercepted the Tic Tac object and witnessed it with her own eyes.

Since the now famous *NY Times* article, we have seen a significant change in how the United States Armed Forces and the US government are handling the UFO topic. On June 25, 2021, the Office of the Director of National Intelligence released a public report titled, "Preliminary Assessment: Unidentified Aerial Phenomena," which promised an ongoing effort to both categorize UFO sightings and try to explain what they are. In this report, they collected 144 reports of UFOs seen in or around military installations. Of those reports, they could not readily explain

143 of those reports. Yes, you read that right. They could explain 1 of those cases.

This stunning admission was highlighted in May of 2022 with a historic congressional hearing on UFOs by the US House Intelligence Counterterrorism, Counterintelligence, and Counterproliferation Subcommittee. After these hearings, it was clear more work had to be done on investigating UFO reports over military airspace and beyond. This would morph into a new office within the Department of Defense, called the All-domain Anomaly Resolution Office (AARO). While this new office promises "resolutions," little if any of the information and data collected will be made public. In fact, when speaking to former Pentagon spokesperson Susan Gough, I was assured that in order to "maintain operations security and to avoid disclosing information that may be useful to our adversaries, DOD does not discuss publicly the details of either the observations or the examination of reported incursions into our training ranges or designated airspace, including those incursions initially designated as UAP."

On January 12, 2023, the Office of the Director of National Intelligence released the unclassified version of the 2022 Annual Report on Unidentified Aerial Phenomena. Under the direction of the newly established ARRO office, the report stated, "In addition to the 144 UAP reports covered during the 17 years of UAP reporting included in the Office of the Director of National Intelligence (ODNI) preliminary assessment, there have been 247 new reports and another 119 that were either since discovered or reported after the preliminary assessment's time period. This totals 510 UAP reports as of August 30, 2022." The report would then go on to state that, "Some of these uncharacterized UAP appear to have demonstrated unusual flight characteristics or performance capabilities, and require further analysis."

While the UFO and UAP acronyms continue to bounce around the halls of Congress and in and out of the Department of Defense, the true nature of these unexplained sightings continues to feed a narrative within the government of threats to national security. Or perhaps even more unnerving, from a militaristic perspective, more highly advanced surveillance and spying technology and possible weaponry from foreign powers. This became no more evident than the 2023 shoot-downs of "unidentified objects" that were discovered over the United States and Canada. To this day, it has still not been disclosed to the public what these objects were.

Despite all of the aforementioned momentum within the United States government on the UFO/UAP topic, there continues to be a seismic gap between UFO sightings within the military apparatus and those occurring in the civilian world. This book attempts to bridge that gap, highlighting both civilian sightings and military sightings, showing that at the very core of each incident is a human being experiencing something they can't explain. And in those rare moments of immediacy and vulnerability, many of those witnesses felt more human than ever before.

In relation to civilian UFO reports, by merely pursuing these reports compiled by independent organizations such as NUFORC and speaking with representatives at both NARCAP and MUFON, it became painfully clear that civilian reports more than double those officially reported by military personnel. While this is mostly because of the ratio of civilians to military personnel, the more important aspect is how these reports are handled by the media that chooses to cover such reports. Military encounters are often covered by local and national news outlets in a very serious manner, while civilian reports are almost never publicized. And if they are, it's usually covered at the very end of a news segment with either a condescending tone or flat-out ridicule. It's no wonder people don't come forward with their UFO sightings when they know they could still suffer the slings and arrows of stigma and ridicule.

This is why I started the *Witness Accounts* series. To give a voice and platform to those who wanted to speak up and speak out. And the snowball effect grew and grew, and more and more people felt empowered to come forward and tell their stories, where they would have the freedom to be as personal and detailed as they wished. More importantly, they are afforded an opportunity to speak their truth for the greater truth that seems to always remain "out there."

This book is broken up into three sections: sightings, close encounters, and military incidents. The first section covers a vast array of UFO sightings from across the world, where individuals looked up into the sky and saw something they couldn't explain. Each of them reflects on the sighting and where they stand on it today. The second section arguably intensifies as we hear stories where individuals claim to have come much more up close and personal with these anomalous phenomena. Some even claim that they may have come into contact with the possible occupants or intelligences behind these phenomena or craft. The third and final section brings us back the military side of things. These individuals share their accounts of UFO sightings and encounters that all occurred while they were on duty at their respective military bases, solidifying that these events could possibly pose a national security threat in the most phenomenal of ways. And just like those in the civilian world, some of these stories are being told for the very first time.

In a rapidly changing world full of incredible scientific discoveries, this also comes with a responsibility to know when science can be implemented into the study of UFOs. When methodical and repeatable data sets can be used to explain UFO events in conventional terms. This approach is necessary to truly and fully understand the vast array of phenomena we seem to be experiencing in our skies. But this book isn't a call to arms to explain the stories you will hear. It is simply, yet if true, a profoundly extensive collection of UFO stories. My sincere hope is that the *Witness Accounts* series of the *Somewhere in the Skies* podcast, along with this book, will both remain a safe space for anyone wanting to share their stories. Stories of those who looked up into the skies, just as I had so many years ago, and witnessed something truly extraordinary. Something that defied everything we thought we knew about the world and the universe. Something that inevitably made us wonder, while also making us remember who we are, where we come from, and why we are here. And perhaps one day, we will all be given a glimpse into the heart of this enduring mystery. A mystery that makes us feel more human. A mystery that sends us on a journey to truly find each other in a world of infinite possibilities. But most importantly: a journey to also find ourselves.

PREFACE

*The following stories come directly from
the transcripts of audio submissions to the
Somewhere in the Skies podcast. Stories have
been edited for structure and clarity.*

Part One

- SIGHTINGS -

The following stories include sightings of UFOs and anomalous phenomena that were seen in our skies throughout the decades. The stories span continents and come from people in all walks of life. Yet they have one thing in common: no explanation for what they had witnessed, even up until today. And as you'll see, it impacted them all in various ways. While patterns can be drawn in terms of the actual objects or phenomena sighted, the uniqueness and diversity of each observer remains at the forefront of each story. Imagine yourself in their shoes, planted firmly on the ground, as they looked up and saw something that was anything but grounded. These are their sightings. Their stories. And these are the ways in which their lives were drastically affected by these events, whether they liked it or not.

AT THE EDGE OF THE LAKE

M y name is Judy Thompson. I am fifty-seven years old, have been married for thirty-six years to my wonderful husband, Bruce, and we have three amazing grown boys. I am a teacher and self-taught artist.

My sighting occurred at Upper Mann Lake, near a small town in northeastern Alberta, Canada, called Ashmont. It is unfortunate that I do not have an exact date, as I was only fourteen years old at the time and did not document anything about the event. The best estimation I can make is that the event took place in the spring, summer or fall of 1980.

I had recently started driving with my newly acquired learner's license. The car I was driving was my grandfather's old Buick LeSabre. On this particular day, I had three passengers; my mom was up front with me in the passenger seat. My grandmother and younger brother, John (ten years old), were sitting in the back seat. Our destination was Ashmont, which was about three miles from our acreage home at Upper Mann Lake. It was the place to go to for minor necessities, as it had a small convenience store.

It was a bright, clear day. It was not foggy, rainy, dusk, dawn, or dark. We were driving back from town, and I slowed down at a sharp bend in the road where there was a small, blue building (a pump house) at the edge of the lake. As I slowed down at the bend in the road, I noticed a black triangular object beyond the pump house, up high in the sky, hovering motionless over the lake. I pulled the car over to the side of the road to get a better look and blurted out something like, "What the heck is that? A UFO?"

I rolled down my window to have a better look while trying to make sense of what this could possibly be. My first thought was that maybe it could be a helicopter with some flat structure hanging under it. It was the only way I could make some kind of sense of something hovering in midair. But helicopters make a lot of noise. This made none. I looked at it for a short time and decided to continue driving. I was worried about the possibility of traffic coming down the narrow road with me parked on the side of the road. I was being a careful and conscientious new driver. I was also worried about frightening my mom and grandmother about what I had blurted out. I knew that they would not be open to things like UFOs. However, I could not stop thinking about the curious/strange object and was wishing I would have looked at it a bit longer.

I continued to drive through our subdivision until I reached the approach to our acreage home. I don't know why I stopped at the approach and looked over my left shoulder, out the driver's side window and up into the sky, but I did. And there it was.

It was a triangular craft. And it was directly over the road, almost as if it had followed us. But now it was just a little higher than the treetops. I quickly put the car in park and shut off the engine. I wanted to hear, once again, if it made any noise. Nothing.

I felt a sense of excitement—not fear. I had another chance to look at this strange object. I got out of the car, leaving the driver door open, and gazed up at the craft hovering silently above me. No one else got out of the car, and no one spoke a word. The craft was not black, but a dull charcoal gray in color. It had no visible lights. It was a perfect triangular shape. It was about thirty feet across. The bottom of the craft had sections/patterns/designs of some type, but I cannot remember. I sure wish I had drawn a sketch of what I saw that day or, better yet, had a camera with me. I wanted to see if it had any windows or identifiable markers, so I walked around to the front of the car and to the other side to get a better view. The sides/front/top were smooth and solid with no windows, markers, or seams of any kind.

As I was standing and gazing up at the craft, I felt a sense of awe and wonder, and I became aware of what felt like my thoughts being read. This may sound really weird, and I would probably leave this part out if it were not for the fact that I have come across other people's accounts of having similar experiences. I had a strong sense that this was an amazing event and that this craft was not of our world. I wanted them (whoever they were) to know that I was greatly honored to have had the chance of a lifetime to witness something so amazing. I began to think about what the occupants may look like, and for the first time I felt a sense of fear creeping in. I don't know if that was the reason, but the craft started to move, gracefully gliding like it was on a sheet of ice.

It first moved a little forward in the direction of the road; then it gracefully turned on a dime about ninety degrees, now facing east towards the lake. The craft started to move slowly, but then suddenly accelerated and took off in a way that I can only describe as "not of this world." It moved at an unreal rate of speed, all in a split second. There was no sound, no smoke, no fire, and no lights. And with that, it was just... gone! The leaves of the tall poplar trees that surrounded the area were completely undisturbed.

I never spoke of the event to anyone, not even my family, for many years. The fear of ridicule was too strong, as I had just started going to a new school. It was not until 2009, while recovering from surgery, that I really began my journey into some serious research on the topic and was hooked. This is when my search for answers began.

It is interesting to note that St. Paul, Alberta, the larger town that is twenty minutes away from where the sighting occurred, is the location of the world's first "UFO Landing Pad." It was built in 1967, the year that the Honorable Paul Hellyer (Canada's Defence Minister at the time) came to St. Paul and dedicated it to the community to celebrate the Canadian Centennial.

This up-close sighting probably only lasted a few minutes. But the impact of the experience will stay with me for the rest of my life. I give the event credit for opening my mind to higher levels of consciousness. I am a critical thinker and do not follow the "crowd." I am aware of the urgency for change in our world today. I am always searching for answers, and realize the importance of truth, peace, love and our connection to Mother Earth.

ORBS ABOVE, DOWN UNDER

My name is Brett Moffatt. I wear a few hats for work, but I mostly work as an instructional designer. I also have a professional fine arts and photography practice, including degrees in teaching and visual arts. I am forty-seven years old, and I live in the Gold Coast in Australia. The Gold Coast is a city with a population of around 680,000 people, and as the name suggests, is on the east coast of Australia, bordering the states of Queensland and New South Wales.

This event took place in 2011. It was about 9 p.m. It was a dark evening, and there was very little moonlight. The sky was clear, and there was no wind. At the time, I was taking a bag of garbage out to a larger bin that we have around the side of the house that faces the southeast.

As I walked via the property's front to go around the house's side, at about a seventy-five-degree angle to the horizon and to the south was an object moving slowly across the sky from east to west at roughly five hundred to seven hundred feet. It moved at a steady pace of perhaps twenty to thirty kilometers per hour, which translates to ten to fifteen knots or twelve to eighteen miles per hour. Beneath it, it had three round orbs of red color equidistant apart in an equilateral triangle. The orbs had a steady red glow, and within each of the orbs was another darker-colored orb. But it was also reddish in the center. The orbs were fairly close to each other, but not that far apart. The red glow had the intensity of an electric hot plate turned on high. It was tough to tell how big or what shape the object was because it was dark, and I could only see the orbs. The orbs appeared to be a part of the same structure, so they didn't appear to be separately moving objects. I would suggest the object was thirty feet in diameter or possibly more, but I'm obviously only guessing.

The object held a steady course in altitude for the entire time I watched it, which lasted for about five minutes or so. The object also emitted a very unusual sound. If you can imagine the sound of gas inside a gas bottle. When you turn a gas bottle on or off, it emits a kind of crackling sound, and the sound was contained within something, as though it was metallic. It was like an echo coming from within a metallic object.

When I first saw the object, I immediately thought it was a fancy Chinese lantern. And although not dismissive, I kind of didn't really think too much of it because I thought, "Oh, that's really cool!" But after about ten seconds, and having heard the sound it was making and by its size, trajectory, course, and altitude, I began to doubt that very quickly. I'm not aware of Chinese lanterns making that kind of sound, and I have no doubt that this object was making that sound. There was no wind either, yet the object retained a steady path and wasn't gaining in altitude. There was no flickering at all from the orbs, either. It was a solid, constant glow. I didn't consider it a drone either because drones were quite rare in Australia in 2011, and the sound it made was entirely different from a drone.

I considered grabbing my phone or camera, but I thought it might disappear when I got back to where I was. So the next morning, I looked up any local headlines on the internet, and there was nothing. I went to work and asked the small team of four people I worked with if anyone had heard of anything in the news about a possible UFO or if any of them had seen anything. No one did. They all listened and took it quite seriously when I told them what I had experienced. They asked the same kinds of questions that I asked myself, and then one of them cracked a joke, and everyone laughed. That was kind of the end of the discussion.

I didn't speak about it much after that, mainly because I didn't think reporting it would have any consequence. Unless someone stepped forward and announced that they had constructed this thing and could explain what it was, then there was no telling what it was. We can only guess. Although I still don't know what I saw, and am reluctant to say I saw a UFO or UAP, I do fervently believe in the phenomena. While I can't rule out that some UFO sightings are the products of US black-budget projects, I am reasonably certain that unidentified aerial phenomena of unknown origins are visiting us. What they are, how they get here, and who or what controls them are the big unanswered questions. And this is what drives my curiosity and desire to study them.

BOY SCOUTS, WICCANS, AND THE NEW JERSEY TRIANGLE

My name is Tom Thompson. I host the podcast *Zero* and the Cortex Zero YouTube channel. I'm a guitarist, artist, and own a small digital design company. I've been researching UFOs for over twenty-five years. These are two of my personal stories of my experiences with the phenomenon that significantly intensified my interest throughout my life.

When I was nine years old, I was in the Boy Scouts. I was on my very first camping trip ever on this particular evening, and I was in the process of earning my fire badge. So when everyone called it a night, two of us would tend to the campfire and make sure it was out. One of the adults would then check the fire, just to be on the safe side, and we would receive our badges if it was completely out.

It had been a pretty interesting night, considering we had a campground right next to us that was occupied by a group of Wiccans. I'm not sure what they were out there for, but at the time, it felt like some kind of celebration. I remember the chanting and singing coming from their camp. It was really beautiful and carried on into the early morning hours.

After tending to the fire and earning our badges, one of my friends and I decided to stay up a bit later, excited over the fact that we technically had no designated bedtime that we had to abide by. I had exited my tent, which was occupied by myself and three of my friends. We sat down on the logs around where the campfire had been, just talking.

The camp was situated in this nice clearing in the woods, surrounded by a tree line that broke apart to reveal a circular section of the sky. This was in the middle of Lebanon State Forest, now known as Brendan T. Byrne State Forest, in Southern New Jersey. It was a clear and bright spring evening, into early morning, cloudless with the stars prominently displayed above us.

My friend and I were sitting there for maybe a half hour or so, just talking, when out of nowhere, there was just this *whoosh,* a pushing of air all around us. It didn't feel like a natural breeze, though. It almost had the quality of a car driving past you at a high speed. And as I took notice of this, I felt the hairs on my body stand up. It was this remarkably weird static electrical sensation, as if I were sitting next to a giant latex rubber balloon. Just a few seconds after, I couldn't help but notice that the usual noises of the outdoors were now nonexistent. It didn't make any sense that all the various wildlife around us would simultaneously fall silent. But it did. And that was when it happened.

In my peripheral vision, to my upper right above, something started protruding from that section of the sky. It slowly moved further into view until the entire object was visible. It was enormous. The moon was exceptionally bright on this night, so there was no misidentifying it. It obscured the stars behind it, and that was when I knew it was a solid craft. It was triangular, with this deep beautiful, yet featureless matte black texture. Each corner of the triangle came to a sort of rounded point. There weren't any discernible rivets or lines of any kind. It wasn't moving very fast. It was comparable to a ship out on calm seas.

I can't stress enough the immense size of this object. Enough that it filled a significant portion of the chunk of sky that was available to us over the clearing we were in. It couldn't have been more than a few hundred feet over the top of the trees. My friend and I didn't say a word, and we didn't make a single move. I remember being so mesmerized by the triangle that it was almost as if my brain was on autopilot.

The craft came to a very slow stop in the direct center of the clearing overhead. On each corner of this craft were three lights in succession, starting from the very front of the object, moving to the left and then the right, just flickering on in a strange fade-in sort of fashion. It was kind of like a smart phone when you hit your power button and the screen fades out, but in reverse. The quality of the lights were gorgeous. They were white, but they all had this almost aqua-blue haze around them. It was just one of the most beautiful things I've ever seen.

I was finally able to speak. And all I could say to my friend was something along the lines of, "Oh my God! What is that? Are you seeing that? Am I imagining this?"

I just wanted to be sure. I needed that verbal confirmation from my friend. But he was badly freaked out, and all he could say was, "I see it. I see it." He just kept stuttering the same phrase over and over, like someone who had been out in the cold for too long. He was physically more frightened than I was, trembling. He actually stood up and was sort of pacing back and forth while keeping his gaze on this gigantic black triangle.

The craft began to move again. As it did, we felt that unnatural electromagnetic sensation escalate. The craft made its way across the sky again and then disappeared over the trees.

The hairs on my body ceased to stand on end, accompanied by yet another unnatural rush of air. About five seconds after, we could no longer see the triangle. The noises one would expect to hear out in the woods at night returned to their natural state.

Now after an event like this, you would expect kids of our age to wake everyone up, screaming and shouting about what had happened. But we just didn't. That sticks out when I recall this event. We went back to the tent, and I don't think we slept very much, but we just didn't talk about it the rest of the night.

Considering I already knew so much about the phenomenon, even at such a young age, the stigma associated with the subject prevented me from sharing the story with almost anyone for several years. As I've gotten older though, I have shared it on several occasions. I have lived with this experience as one of the driving factors in me researching the phenomenon and related subjects. This happened to me, and there's no changing that fact. It changed everything. I went from a believer to an experiencer. I still get chills when I sit and picture that triangular craft gliding through the sky.

I'm left with really only two possibilities, as far as what it was: black military or aerospace tech of the highest order... or nonhuman intelligence. The technology required to get that thing off the ground, let alone maneuver it through the air, didn't exist, at least publicly, in 1998. Nor does it exist now in 2023.

There have been moments of internalized frustration associated with sharing my experience. Mostly stemming from relaying it to the closed-minded among us. I get it, though. I can't help but wish they could have seen what I did and felt everything that I felt when this event happened. The experience altered the trajectory of my entire existence. I'm just a guy looking for answers to the most profound questions we have asked as a species. I am relentless in this search. I live with the knowledge that something is happening, and it's a double-edged sword like almost nothing else.

My second experience happened on November 26, 2022. This event caught me completely off guard; even though it was not the first time this type of thing has taken place in my life, it takes nothing away from the sheer awe I found myself in as I laid eyes on something I could not explain floating in the sky above me.

At approximately 2 p.m., I was driving my work truck, heading east in the direction of my job, to return from doing field visits. Ironically, only ten minutes prior to this, I had been recording a vlog video on the phenomenon. As I approached the intersection where I would be taking a left turn, there was a sharp bright glimmer that caught my eye above me through the windshield. I looked upward, and there it was in the sky. Above my truck was this cone just sitting in place. Yet it was rotating, not very fast, but just turning in a circular motion. The top portion of the cone came to a sharp point. With the sun to its right, it glistened almost like metal. But it had a very glassy, translucent appearance.

The blue sky was clear of any real cloud cover, so I had the object in full direct view. It was a beautiful thing to lay eyes on. My sense of time began to waver. Not to mention the fact that I had to keep my eyes on the road. The sighting lasted for what I estimate to be the slowest three seconds I've ever experienced. And then it vanished. But not a split-second flash or anything like that. It was as if the object took the sky behind it and wrapped it around itself like a sheet and faded behind it.

At this point, my phone was now in my hand, with my camera on and ready. However, it had transpired too quickly for me to even have a chance of capturing anything. But just in case the object decided to show itself one more time, I pulled over into the parking lot directly to my right and began to record. I waited for about ten minutes or so, but to no avail.

I was stunned. It really took me by surprise, ironically appearing just after I had recorded a video talking about the phenomenon. It was as if I was being teased by whatever the intelligence was behind this event. After I stopped the recording, I got back into my truck, and I began recording a different clip. In this clip, I made note of my location, the time, the date, and the quick details of what I had seen. Not too long after that, I returned to my job, and I filed a report with the National UFO Reporting Center (NUFORC). I provided as detailed a description as possible.

It really kills me that the object, whatever it was, vanished before I even had the slightest chance to capture it on video, or at least a photo. Regardless, I was grateful to have seen such a beautiful and mysterious sight.

The rest of the week was pretty odd for me too. I'm not sure if these events are related, but I still wanted to make note of anything out of the ordinary, because this is how the phenomenon seems to operate, based on what I know of it. That week, every single night, my dreams were dramatically lucid.

Just out of nowhere on the twenty-eighth, two days after the sighting, the way my day began was extremely unusual, following yet another lucid dream. When I got up out of bed... and I've never had this type of feeling to such an extraordinary degree, I was questioning whether or not I was still asleep. It was really odd. I've had that kind of thing last for maybe a few seconds in bed before getting up plenty of times prior, but this stopped me in my tracks and lasted fifteen minutes or so. Again, I don't really know if there's any direct correlation between my sighting and this unusual sleep pattern and subsequent incident of my mind questioning my surroundings, but I feel it was more than worth noting.

That's not all, though. On three separate occasions over that next week, I experienced what I can only describe as precognition.

I am not claiming to be some kind of mystic here. And I have my own personal opinions on such phenomena. But this really couldn't be ignored. And during meditation, I had been experiencing very strange presences around me, very similar to the feeling that you'll get when someone enters the room you're in and you haven't even laid eyes on them yet.

In the months following the sighting, it felt like my life had entered a beautiful new chapter. So many wonderful things have begun to happen, and I can't help but feel as though that cone in the sky may have been a sign of the great things that have now come to fruition. There is no way for me to know whether or not that's true.

All I truly know is that we know very little.

GET YOUR OWN DAMN CIGARETTES!

My name is Ron Zlotnik. I'm originally from a little town called Windsor, in Ontario, Canada. Nothing really big comes out of Windsor, making it a little difficult to find a lot of UFO reports from there. But here are two of my stories.

This happened when I was about five or six years old, around 1978. One evening, when the sun was nearly down, I recall a bit of unrest around the neighborhood, when a lot of people were on the street, looking towards our local airport. That was when I saw it. It was an elongated oval-shaped object and was a yellowish, metallic color. I would say it was probably about the size of a couple of 747 jets end to end. It seemed to be kind of hovering over the runway, higher than the air traffic controller tower, but not too much higher. This thing was hovering in a way that it was kind of preventing planes from landing or taking off. It had to have been hovering there for around twenty minutes. No matter what it was, it definitely seemed like something that shouldn't be there.

At this point in my life, there was no internet, and I didn't know about MUFON, so there was no easy way to report this.

People called the local airport, trying to get information. All they said was that they were looking into it. I remember my father ushered me inside our house before I could really see too much more.

This happened around 1984 when I was about thirteen years old. We were living in a different house from my earlier account. Behind my house was a really large field, and it was underdeveloped. Even though we were in the city, on the other side of the field, kind of, was a 7-Eleven store. In that day and age, it wasn't uncommon for parents to send their kids to buy them cigarettes. Yeah... I feel old. My father would regularly send me on runs to grab him cigarettes. I always had my head in the clouds. I'd always be looking up at the night sky when I'd go through this long field. So on this one particular night, when I was more than halfway across the field, I was looking at a wide field of stars, and I noticed a seemingly plain star that had not moved previously and then suddenly started moving and drifting across the sky in a slow, rhythmic fashion. It was sort of like how a modern-day satellite moves in orbit. After a few seconds of that constant motion, it sped up a bit, and then it seemed to traverse about a quarter of the sky. Then it stopped and hovered motionless in place.

At this point, I'd stopped walking, as my gaze was frozen on this little star. It would move and then stop. Move again and then stop again. Still, there was no sound. I watched it for about fifteen seconds, and then I saw the strangest thing. I saw what appeared to be a beam of faint white light slowly grow out of the star. The light kind of reminded me of how like a lightsaber turns on. So it just kind of grew, coming out of that dot, and when it was about an inch long from my perspective on the ground against the length of the sky, the entire beam then started to spin around the central dot, and as it spun, the colors oscillated through all the various colors of the rainbow. But in no particular order of color. It seemed to be just kind of random as it spun around and around and around. It spun around this dot a dozen or so times, and then it abruptly stopped again and slowly retracted into the center of the dot like somebody turned off the lightsaber.

So at this point, I was just completely in shock and awe and frozen in place. About five to ten more seconds passed with nothing happening. And then, that dot just shot off across the sky at, like, warp twenty, and it was gone. That was the end of it. I was completely frozen in place for a couple of minutes after that, just scanning the sky and feeling a little bit shaken, feeling both fear and amazement. Then I finally came to my senses, and with the cigarette money in my hand, I turned around and beelined it back home, came crashing through the door, and threw the money at my father as I ran past him. All I remember is yelling, "Get your own damn cigarettes!" and running into my bedroom and slamming the door shut.

My father was obviously pretty taken by surprise by that. That was definitely not my normal behavior, especially for a thirteen-year-old, so you can imagine he wanted to know what the hell was going on. And I told him. He kind of listened and didn't make too much out of it. But I know in his heart, he knows it was something. Looking back, it seems funny now, but at the time, I was pretty shaken by it, and it definitely solidified my curiosity and interest for a very long time. Needless to say, I didn't get my father cigarettes for a long time after that night!

Based on my life experiences and the curiosities that were sparked inside me by everything I've seen and read up on, my feelings are pretty solid in the matter. There are billions of stars out there, and it's mathematically impossible that we're the only ones. I want to keep religion out of this, but if religion suggests that God created the universe, the heavens, and Earth, and that it should be all there to kind of service us, I have to admit I'm not a strong believer in that philosophy. I'm very much into astrophysics and understanding the metaphysical nature of the universe and the cosmos.

I'm not going to sit here and say, "Yep! UFOs are aliens!" But

I'm certainly not going to discount it either. Is there a current earth-based technology concept, that's proven, that shows faster than light travel, which would be required to traverse the distances even to our closest neighbor star? Not currently. There's certainly philosophical concepts and astrophysical ideas and constructs, but I do believe that considering the universe was created and expanded out, there could definitely be civilizations that were developed millennia ahead of us that may have had a heck of a lot longer to develop technologically. This could allow them to unlock a way to travel this far.

Regardless, those are my feelings on the topic, and that's where I stand... for now.

THE METEOROLOGIST AND THE FOO FIGHTERS

My name is Nicolle Morock, and I host the *P.E.E.P.* podcast. I'm a meteorologist, writer, and podcast producer. This event happened in November of 1997 just south of Falls Lake and north of Raleigh, North Carolina. I was driving home from work down Highway 50, which is a two-lane highway that goes over the lake and through the woods. It was approaching dusk just a little after 5 p.m.

At that time, I was about a year out of college with a communications degree. I was an editor and office manager for a small wedding video company. Back then, there was hardly anything on that road because development hadn't spread that far yet. I was approaching a rare intersection with a stoplight, which was—and still is—in a clearing, and I was heading south. To my left, on the north side of the intersection was a gas station, set back a bit from the road. A tree line was at least fifty feet behind that. There was a man driving the vehicle in front of me, and I was driving my little red pickup truck. The light was red, so we were slowing to a stop.

Something made me look back to my left out my side window. It might have been motion in my side-view mirror, but I'm not sure. I looked over my shoulder as I was stopping, and saw two round balls. These days, I'd call them orbs of light, but at that time I didn't really know that word. They were back to the northeast.

In height, they were close to the top of the tall pine trees we have all over North Carolina. They looked to be about the size of beach balls (bigger than a basketball for sure). I don't recall any solid form, just two lights. And I have to admit all these years later, I'm a little fuzzy on the exact color they started as, but I think it was red. They came from behind me and flew toward the center of the intersection in front of me. As they did, it was like they were playing follow-the-leader. They stayed about four feet apart the whole time, and the one in front changed color when it was parallel to my side of the truck. I think it went to yellow. Just a half-second later—quickly but definitely delayed—the one behind it changed to the same color.

When they got over the intersection, they made a sharp turn and went back to my right (northwest) and headed back toward the trees on that side of the clearing. It all seemed to happen in slow motion, and I remember wondering if the guy in front of me was seeing the same thing. How could he miss it?

The light turned green, and he started driving, so I did, too. I don't recall seeing them appear or disappear. I just watched them as they made this V-shape in the sky above me. It seemed like they got lower as they approached the road and higher as they left. I didn't have to strain my neck to look up through the windshield to see them in front of me. It was obviously weird, but I wasn't scared—just really curious. What on earth did I just see?

I grew up hearing stories of others in my family having seen UFOs, so maybe that's why I didn't freak out. I spent the rest of the drive home—about seven minutes into Raleigh—going over it all in my head. There was nothing attached to the lights. If it had been a helicopter, unless it was completely invisible, I would have seen it, and I'm pretty sure we *still* don't have that kind of technology.

I still lived with my parents at the time and couldn't wait to tell my dad when I got home because I was sure he'd believe me. He did, but of course, he couldn't tell me what it was either.

They reminded me of drones from *Star Wars* even though there's not technically anything like that in *Star Wars*. I'm not convinced they weren't terrestrial, but as a meteorologist, I'm 100% sure it wasn't any type of weather phenomena or "swamp gas." These seemed to be under intelligent control, and their path made the shape of a V over the intersection.

I've met quite a few meteorologists over the years who work in the Department of Defense, US Army, and US Air Force, and I've shared my experience with each one and asked if they had ever heard of or seen anything like that. All have said no. And even the ones with higher clearances have had looks on their faces that said they weren't lying.

I've always been fascinated with the unknown, and this experience just cemented my interest in UAP. I'm not quite obsessed, but I watch as many documentaries as I can and listen to your podcast and others, hoping to hear someone describe something similar. So far, I haven't. Maybe someone out there is waiting to hear my story so they can relate, too.

WHAT VAN GOGH MUST HAVE SEEN

My name is Kelly Chase. I host *The UFO Rabbit Hole* podcast. I saw a UFO when I was thirteen years old. I was on vacation with my family at the Outer Banks in North Carolina, in a little town called Avon just north of Hatteras. We went there almost every summer, and one of my favorite things to do at night was to sit outside and watch the stars. Having grown up in the suburbs where the sky is always a dull shade of orange, and the stars are few and far between, the spectacle of a truly dark night sky filled with thousands of stars was something I couldn't resist. I found myself out on the deck most nights, looking up at the stars in awe.

One particular night, I was out on the deck in my usual stargazing routine when I had the strangest thought go through my head, "What if I see a UFO?" It was a very strange thought. UFOs weren't something that I ever really thought about. Yet, suddenly, I felt the very strong urge to scan the skies, looking for something I wasn't sure that I even really believed existed. And as soon as I did so, I saw a light moving across the sky.

It was a small, bright, clear light that seemed to be moving a little too swiftly to be a plane. And as soon as I locked my eyes onto it, it took a hard ninety-degree turn and then another before accelerating instantaneously and streaking off past the horizon like a meteor.

I remember being absolutely electrified by what I saw. I felt like I was going to crawl out of my skin. I didn't know what I had seen exactly, but I knew that it moved like nothing else that I'd ever seen. Even at thirteen, I knew instinctively that the physics of it all stretched the boundaries of all reason, yet I knew what I had seen.

I ran in the house to tell my family, but they laughed at me and accused me of making up stories. And to be honest, there was a part of me that wondered if maybe I had imagined the whole thing. I mean, how could it be possible that I just happened to see something so strange and seemingly impossible literally a second after having this strange thought that I might see a UFO? Was I fooling myself? I had a pretty active imagination as a kid, but I never had any trouble differentiating my flights of fancy from actual reality. Yet when everyone else thinks that you are making it up, at a certain point it becomes easier to place that doubt with yourself.

I didn't think about the UFO much after that. Probably not even once a year. But every long once in a while I would remember that night and wonder what it was that I had seen.

It wasn't until the spring of 2021 when I returned to the Outer Banks with my family that this story suddenly became top-of-mind for me again. I had been half paying attention to the occasional news story I came across that talked about how the government had admitted that UFOs are real and that we don't know what they are. Each time I came across a story like that, it made me think of what I had seen when I was thirteen, and a little part of me wondered if I might have actually seen a UFO.

And so when my family decided to return to the Outer Banks for vacation, it felt like the perfect time to dive back into the subject and figure out what was going on. I had a whole week with nothing to do but kill time reading on the beach, and I thought that given that time to focus, I'd be able to get to the bottom of what was really going on pretty quickly—mostly because I didn't really believe at that point that UFOs were real. The government was saying that UFOs are real, but the government says a lot of things. I figured this had to be some kind of a play to get a rubber stamp for black-budget spending, or maybe it was secret foreign tech. I wasn't sure what was going on exactly, but I was sure that it had some kind of a rational explanation.

However, instead of a neat and tidy explanation, what I discovered was a deep and labyrinthian rabbit hole where each new mystery, once examined, gave way to an even deeper one, and whose tendrils seemed to be entwined through every academic discipline and sphere of life. There were no easy answers, only a bottomless well of questions. I was utterly fascinated and completely hooked.

So fast-forward a year to the summer of 2022. I'd been working on the podcast for the past nine months and was finding myself deeper and deeper in the world of UFOs. I ended up taking a class from one of my favorite authors on the subject, Dr. Diana Walsh Pasulka. She wrote a book called *American Cosmic* that made a huge impact on me and my understanding of the phenomenon, so I was excited to learn from her.

I learned so much in Diana's class, and one of the most profound things that I learned was about the process of redaction that occurs when someone has an anomalous experience like a UFO sighting. The stigma associated with such events, often paired with serious doubts or outright disbelief that such things are even possible, can cause people to change how they tell the story of what happened to them, even to themselves.

And as I learned about how this redaction process unfolds, I had a startling realization. My UFO sighting at the Outer Banks when I was thirteen wasn't the only sighting I've had. In fact, I had a much more profound sighting in a park outside of Akron, Ohio, in broad daylight when I was twenty-one. Let me first tell that story, and then I'll explain how I think it is that I came to forget that something so extraordinary had happened.

It was a spring day in April of 2007. I'd been going through a tough time, and a friend invited me to a local Metropark. The plan was for us to hang out in the woods and do LSD. I'd never done it before, and to be honest, I had no real idea of what I was getting myself into. We each did one hit and then sat on the top of this hill overlooking a pond surrounded by trees.

After a while, the visuals started kicking in. It wasn't anything major, but for a first-timer it was thrilling. I remember looking at the twisting, yellow-green grass of early spring and thinking that I understood now what Van Gogh must have seen. We sat there talking, having that kind of sweeping, cerebral conversation that flows from such a state. It was a very pleasant and mellow experience.

But at one point during this conversation, something seemed to appear above the tree line. I remember both of us being startled by it, because although it was very large and only a couple of hundred feet above the tree line, it truly seemed to come out of nowhere. We'd both been staring in that direction, but we never saw it approach. It was just there. As though it had emerged from a hole in the sky itself that we couldn't see.

At first I thought it was the Goodyear blimp. Akron, Ohio, is the home of the Goodyear blimp, so seeing it floating overhead was a pretty common occurrence. And this did remind me of the blimp in some ways. It was of a similar size, though this was slightly bigger than the blimp. And the way that it seemed to float slowly and stoically across the sky reminded me of how the blimp moves.

But that was where the similarities ended. Whatever this was was a deep brown color and more oblong in shape than a blimp, what many would call cigar-shaped. Any other details are impossible to give. Although the object had a distinct size and shape, it also somehow felt like it didn't have any discreet edges. It was hard to look at, almost like it was blurry. I kept rubbing my eyes, trying to get the image to resolve into something familiar, but all I saw was this long, brown smudge moving slowly across the sky. It made me weirdly uncomfortable, and I felt like I wanted to look away from it.

And then as quickly as it was there, it was gone. It traveled maybe a few hundred yards across the sky over the tree line and then disappeared as strangely as it had appeared, as if into an unseen hole in the air itself.

My friend definitely saw it, too, and we kept asking each other, "What was that?" And even though we agreed that it didn't look anything like the blimp, we also ultimately agreed that it had to be the blimp. I mean, after all, what else could it have been? And we were, quite literally, tripping. So that must be it, right? What I'd thought I'd seen was impossible, so the only explanation was that I hadn't seen it. And so I simply put it out of my mind.

But how does that happen? I'll admit that even having experienced this whole thing for myself, it's still very strange and unsettling for me to realize that I could just forget something like that, and continue to not remember it, even when I was spending every spare second of my day immersed in the study of the phenomenon. I was thinking about UFOs literally all the time, so how could I have forgotten what I'd seen?

"Forgetting" actually isn't even the right word. Because it's not like this memory was blocked or suppressed exactly. I think that does happen to people, but it didn't feel like that was what happened to me. Rather this felt more like a categorization error of some kind in my brain. It's like that memory was a file in my brain, and because I had never named that file "UFO sighting," when I searched for UFO sightings in my brain, that experience didn't pop up. I hadn't built any connections in my brain between that experience and a UFO sighting, and so, for me, those connections simply didn't exist.

And I think there are a few different reasons for why that happened, all of which I suspect are pretty common among people who have these types of experiences:

First of all, I didn't think of what I saw as a UFO because it didn't look like what I thought a UFO was supposed to look like. As someone who, at that point in my life, didn't have even a casual interest in UFOs, my main conception of the phenomenon was from what I saw in the media. To me, a UFO was a flying saucer. An actual, solid, technological craft piloted by aliens from another planet.

That's just not what this looked like at all. I couldn't really tell what it was. And even though it reminded me vaguely of a blimp, it's weird blurry appearance didn't look like any kind of craft that I'd ever seen, so I didn't necessarily think it was a craft. What I saw defied categorization, so my brain simply failed to categorize it.

The second reason for this categorization error was the fact that we were on LSD. Like I said, that was the first time that I'd ever done LSD, and I didn't really know anything about what that experience was supposed to be like. I'd heard that LSD made you "see things," so I assumed that's what it had done.

However, looking back more than fifteen years later, and with a considerable amount of experience with psychedelics under my belt, I look at this experience differently. For me, LSD can dramatically change the quality of what I'm looking at, things can seem to look alive at the molecular level, colors and textures are more profound, but I've never had an experience on LSD where I saw something that wasn't there, particularly something that another person can also see.

That doesn't mean that I have entirely ruled out that what we saw was just a weird shared visual experience as a result of being chemically altered. It could be. It's just that given my other experiences, it seems unlikely.

It's also changed my perspective to understand that many people who research psychical phenomena and contact experiences see psychedelics as a legitimate contact modality that can allow people to perceive things and tap into abilities that they otherwise wouldn't have access to. We're still learning about what psychedelics do to the brain, but despite the traditional view that they increase activity in the brain, the latest research suggests that psychedelics significantly disrupt normal neural activity and quiet the brain. Could this allow your conscious mind to pick up on things that it otherwise would filter out? It's too early to know for sure, but it's certainly possible.

There was a final reason that I managed to entirely forget this experience, and it's because, frankly, I doubted my own mental state. In the spring of 2007, I was coming out on the other end of what I sincerely hope will end up being the worst year of my life. My father had been diagnosed with a rare and aggressive form of cancer and passed away suddenly, leaving my family devastated. A few days after the funeral, my fiancé cheated on me and abruptly ended our relationship. And then, after months of licking my wounds, I went out on my first date as a single woman with a charming PhD candidate my friends introduced me to, and he ended up drugging and raping me. I apologize for bringing the room down with all of that, but for the purposes of this conversation, I think it's important to make clear the level of trauma that I was processing at the time.

The thing about processing trauma and grief is that it can make you doubt yourself on the most fundamental level. For me, I think it was easier to believe that the tragedies that had befallen me were somehow my fault than it was to deal with what felt like the utter randomness of the universe and its seeming indifference to suffering. At least if it was my fault, then I had some level of control. And hypothetically, if I could fix the things that were wrong with me that caused these things to happen, then I could stop them from happening again.

It doesn't make a lot of rational sense, but it's the kind of Faustian bargain that people deep in grief make all the time. But instead of saving yourself, you end up poisoning yourself with endless self-recriminations. And that's where I was on that spring day in 2007, heartbroken, beaten down, and filled with a deep self-loathing. I didn't trust myself or my perceptions of reality, and I felt awash in a sea of cognitive dissonance. So when I saw something that I didn't think I could possibly have seen, it had never been easier to doubt myself. I just assumed I was wrong.

And the reason I bring this up is because as I have spent more time diving into the experiencer literature, it's clear that trauma, like psychedelics, might at times provide a window into experiences and perceptions that we wouldn't normally have. No one knows why this is exactly. Perhaps it's just that the psychologically destabilizing impact of these events allows things to get through your filters that normally wouldn't. Again, we don't know.

But I wanted to share my story because I don't think it's unusual. I wasn't the only person in Dr. Pasulka's class who uncovered anomalous experiences in their past that had been redacted and pruned past the point of all recognition. But once you understand how this process of redaction works, and the motives that underlie the personal misreporting of our own experiences, it becomes a very simple task to excavate those experiences and reintegrate them back into the fabric of your life.

Which is not the same thing as finding answers. I still have no idea what I saw at the beach that night when I was thirteen. And I feel like I have even less of a sense of what I saw at the park when I was twenty-one. And I may never know.

But I am grateful for the fullness of life that is available on the other side of redaction. Instead of forcibly amputating the experiences that I can't explain, I'm able to make room for them. Allowing for mystery to exist and carving out a place in my psyche for the unknowable has brought a sense of depth, meaning, and awe back into my life that I thought I'd lost in childhood. And best of all, I'm no longer at war with myself or my memories. And in reestablishing that trust with myself, I've found a great deal of peace.

THAT UNIDENTIFIED FLYING FERRIS WHEEL

My name is Andy McGrillen. I host *That UFO Podcast*. In 2019, I saw a black triangle while coming home along a dark, but busy road in Northumberland in the United Kingdom. It was about 6 p.m., so everyone was coming home from work. That was when I noticed two lights low down in the sky, maybe a couple of hundred feet off the ground. This was near an airport, so I just thought that it was a plane coming in. But it was on an odd path, given that the runways were farther away. I also noticed that as I drove towards it, it wasn't moving at all. It was stationary, just hovering in the sky. No flashing of the lights. Nothing.

I noticed that this white van had pulled over to the side of the road, and the gentleman driving the van was leaning out and looking up. As I drove underneath the lights, I could clearly make out, against the black winter sky, a black triangular shape. The two lights strangely were just at the back of the object, and there was nothing on the front. Going under it, I expected to see the outline of an aircraft or the other lights at the tail or the front. But there was nothing. Just the two lights on the tip. And again, this thing was completely still. I managed to turn the car around, and as I did, I looked in my rearview mirror, and the object moved over some trees diagonally. Just a really strange kind of movement.

I turned the car around and back along the road. And there was this clearing that opened up to an expansive field where I had a clear view of the sky. And given this thing was only a couple of hundred feet at most off the ground, you would have been able to see it. And I couldn't. It was gone. That was my second sighting. My first was much more interesting.

This happened in the mid-'90s in Glasgow, Scotland. I'm not too exact on the year, but it would have been October or November, as I remember it was very cold and dark. I would have been about nine or ten years old. There were five of us leaving what would be the Boys' Brigade, which is a bit like the Boy Scouts in the States. It was my mum, sister, a friend of mine, his mum, and myself. We were leaving the church where the Boys' Brigade would meet.

We were walking along this road. To the right, about a half a mile away, there was a very built-up suburban area. Lots of houses, shops, lights, and traffic. And as I look down the street, behind this tree line, there was this object. The only way I can really describe it is if you imagine a Ferris wheel you would see at a carnival. But it was slightly tilted at an angle. And it was spinning around ridiculously quick like a washing machine cylinder.

I could just make out these lights. I can't say it was definitely disc-shaped. But given the angle it was at, and the fact it was spinning, it seemed like it was some sort of circular-type object. And we all saw it. It was no more than a few seconds before we started walking away, and it was soon out of view. And that was it.

I still remember it to this day, and it definitely turned me on to a lifelong passion and interest. It was honestly the most spectacular thing I've ever seen.

A LEAF ON THE WIND

My name is Dan Zetterström. This sighting took place on the morning of June 8, 2021, in Barry in South Wales. The weather at the time was 10 degrees Celsius, and it was completely clear skies. The property where this happened was a small bungalow with a garden. I could see this huge swath of sky, with nothing to block it. And I watched a plane go by, and it took about ten minutes for it to clear my view. That will play in to this later on.

Just to preface this story, after this experience, I checked satellite trackers, and I checked plane trackers. I checked everything. And even though I kind of knew from the movement that we didn't make things that move that way, I still thought that it was important to check these things.

I was sat outside, looking up at a clear sky, and I asked for something to happen. About five seconds later, this enormous owl flew over. Owls are usually a sign of high strangeness. In this case, I wouldn't have thought anything of it if what was about to happen didn't happen.

I asked for a bigger event to happen. A moment later, five

more owls of the same size flew over the top of me in a V-formation. It was wild.

A few moments later, I looked upwards, I took a deep breath, and I gave gratitude to the universe. And at that very moment, I saw a star move in right near where I was looking. It wasn't moving in any crazy way, It was just kind of steadily moving from north to south. And when it got to the highest point above me, it just stopped. And it stopped for long enough that it got my attention. Up until that moment, I thought that maybe it was a satellite. But clearly, it wasn't.

The light hung in the night sky for a while. I asked it for something impressive. At that point, I did a double take, because the movement that it started making just wasn't movement that any craft that I know of would make. Imagine a leaf falling on the wind. Swooshing side to side, getting lower and lower. From the highest point in the sky, it drifted downwards like a leaf on the wind to the horizon. Just as it was about to disappear over the roof of the house, the object shot from south to north and covered the space that it took the commercial plane about ten minutes in about three seconds!

And then... it was gone.

Whatever this was, it simply was not ours. Or at least something that doesn't use propulsion or move in the same way as we are used to seeing. The left-right swinging motion was just wild to witness. As soon as I sat down, slack-jawed and mind blown about what just happened, I once again gave gratitude to the universe and said, "Thank you." I did a little bit of meditation, and as soon as I opened my eyes, four more owls flew over me!

There's just no other word to describe the experience other than "majestic." It took me from a believer to knower. This thing was anomalous. This thing was extremely likely to not be ours. It was just a very impressive and life-changing experience.

THE ADIRONDACK EGG

My name is Rob Kristoffersen. I host the *Our Strange Skies* podcast. I have lived all my life in the Adirondack Park of northern New York. It's a quiet, picturesque kind of place. If there's one town that stands out, just by reputation, it's Lake Placid just because it was the site of the "Miracle on Ice" in 1980. Other than that, the area is kind of unremarkable. It's beautiful in its landscape. You're surrounded by mountains. You're surrounded by trees, and it's a lot of beauty to take in, really. And where I live, it's a very dark and secluded place. It's a town of about five thousand people, there isn't a ton of light pollution up there, and the town even has its own observatory.

In June of 2015, I was working my job doing laundry at a nursing home. It was about 10:30 a.m., and a friend had come down to grab me to go out for a break. At first, I turned him down because I had a lot of work to do. But the room where I work is very stuffy all the time, so I decided I would go out with him to get some fresh air.

Where we take our breaks is technically off the property.

Because the nursing home is under hospital rules, you can't smoke on the actual property. So we're standing on this corner, and

there's a house adjacent to us. We're just talking and shooting the breeze. And all of a sudden, I just looked up. It was bright blue skies that day. Not a cloud up there. But there was this really strange object up there.

If I had to describe it, it would be as if you took an egg, turned it on its side, and blew it up, like, three hundred times the size of what a normal egg would be. Very large. The way it was in the air was like if you threw it up there and you somehow got it to stick and fly. That's literally what it looked like. It had a white color to it. It wasn't reflective at all, and it was moving parallel to where we were standing. It was moving at such a slow pace.

We both looked up at it, and we just stood there. That was the odd thing. We didn't jump around proclaiming, "Hey, look at this UFO! Hey, everybody... get a look at this UFO!" That's not what happened. We just stood there, and we watched it as it continued moving at that slow pace, parallel to where we were standing. It didn't seem like it was at a high elevation, but I really couldn't be too sure.

I didn't want to take a picture of it. I can't wrap my head around that to this day. Why didn't we want to take a picture of this? Was it doing something to us that made us calm? That made us not even think about taking a picture? We both had phones on us, yet neither of us took a picture. It was so weird. I still ruminate on that to this day.

The object was moving closer to where we were. And then, all of a sudden, it stopped in midair, turned a full ninety degrees, and then started flying away from us at the same slow pace. Whatever it was, it was kind of nonchalant. It did what it wanted to do.

To this day, I don't know how to describe this experience. I haven't talked to my friend in a long time, but I've always wanted to get in touch with them again and talk about this. There's something deeper to this experience that I don't yet know. But that sighting has had a lasting impact on me. I read UFO books all the time. I have a UFO podcast. I think about UFOs and what they are, why they're here, and why people see them. I think about this stuff all the time because some egg-shaped object was in the sky one day, and I happened to see it.

A BIRTHDAY SURPRISE

My name is Luis Jimenez. I'm an actor in Los Angeles, California, and I also host the YouTube channel Lu Reviews. I'm very fascinated by the UAP topic, and this is my story.

It was 1993. I was thirteen years old. I was living in Cooper City, Florida, about twenty miles outside of Miami. My best friend at the time, Tony, invited me to a birthday party that summer of one of his friends. Now, I can't remember this girl's name, but what I do remember is that she didn't live very far from me. I'd say probably two miles tops. But, again, my house was in one of these very cookie-cutter developments, but her house was lined up against an entire cow pasture.

So we got to this party. It was a great time. Typical kids birthday party. But there was a lot of people. This family had a lot of friends. The sun went down, and the party was still going on. At some point, Tony and I saw this girl who was standing out in the middle of this property, and she was by herself. It turned out that it was actually the girl whose party it was. And she was looking to the sky. We were wondering what she was doing, so we walked over there and asked her what she was looking at. She pointed up and that was when we saw it.

We both looked up and saw a strange light. It was pretty high, and it was pretty far away. Nothing crazy unusual about it. But the next thing I remember is that this light was hovering a hundred feet or so above this cow pasture. It was like the size of two school buses if they were stacked on top of one another. I remember it having a shape. When I explain it to people, I often describe it as like a breakfast bowl you would put your cereal in. Imagine if you took that breakfast bowl and just made it one tenth smaller and then you take that bowl and you flip it on top of the one sitting on the table. You put them together at the rim, and that's kind of what this thing looked like. What I really remember is how bright it was. Especially in the middle. It was so bright. The outside aura of it was almost like a green hue.

By this time, the entire party had walked over to where we were. You could hear various people saying things like, "Wow... Oh my God!" and "What is that!? What's going on!?" It was almost like slow motion. Even as a thirteen-year-old kid, I can remember going through my mental rolodex of what this object could be. Helicopter? No. There was no noise. It was close enough, so we should have heard something. Was it a blimp? No. It wasn't big enough to be a blimp. We have the Goodyear Blimp in this area of Florida all the time, or something going on in Fort Lauderdale or Miami that requires a Goodyear Blimp. So I was very familiar with blimps. *This* was not a blimp. It couldn't have been a plane because it was stationary. Also, what would a plane be doing above a cow pasture? Nothing that I could think of was matching what I was looking at.

I wanted to get a better look at this thing, so I began running toward this object. I got to this dirt road that was close to the cow pasture. The road had these really tall pine trees that lined it, and I did not take my eyes off this object. However, I did lose it behind these trees. And the second I got to the dirt road, I lost track of it. Once I got to the actual road and looked up beyond the trees, it was gone. I never saw it again. I was floored.

As a kid, I had already had an interest in UFOs. As a matter of fact, the very first thing that got me into the UFO topic was the Bob Lazar story, which had happened four years earlier. So my curiosity about this topic had already been fueled. I was already looking at UFO books in the library as well. So that's why I think I was in a very unique position to witness something like this, because I'd already had a frame of reference.

This incident was profound in the way it made me feel. I've never been that excited to have seen something in my life. I think it did scare some people at the party, but I was really excited because I knew what I was looking at was a UFO. I wish I had stayed where I was, because then maybe I would have been able to see it take off or blink out or whatever happened. But I never got the opportunity to see that.

So that night when I got home from the party, I burst through the front door at a million miles per hour. My entire family was there. My sister, my little brother, my mother, my grandmother, my stepdad... they were all pretty much sleeping at this point. But I ran into my parents' bedroom, and I was just so excited and so amped. I wanted them to hop out of bed and listen to what I was saying because my life had just profoundly changed, and I wanted them to know why! But... my parents did not react the way I had hoped for. It was more like, "Okay, son. Let's talk about it tomorrow. We're just trying to get some sleep..."

I didn't sleep at all that night. As a matter of fact, what was interesting is that at the time, there was this television show on Fox where you could call in and tell your stories of seeing UFOs. So I did! I laid out every single detail in a voice message to the production company. So maybe somewhere out there, there's a recording of my testimony on what happened.

I can't stress enough how profound a moment this was in my life. And ever since then, I've been absolutely hooked. I've gone down the rabbit holes, and I've worked my way out of rabbit holes. And the cool thing is that it's taken me twenty-seven years to really formulate and learn how to talk about this experience. But not only this experience, but my passion for the UFO field.

I would kill to go back in a time machine and relive that summer night in 1993. It is a badge of honor that I got to witness something that very few people have ever experienced. And I feel lucky. I really do.

THE GOLD COAST TRIANGLE

My name is Jamie-lee Ryan, and I live in the Gold Coast, Australia. My sighting took place on July 14 in 2021 at around 5 p.m. I just want to preface this by saying that I've always believed in UFOs and aliens and am fascinated by the topic.

As a kid, I grew up in a small country town in Australia somewhat in the outback. There wasn't much to do apart from going camping. A lot of the time, we'd be at sleepovers and out on the trampoline, looking at the stars. So I've looked at the skies most of my life, and I've never seen anything apart from your normal satellite. Until this one day.

It was a normal workday for me. I work from home, and I usually finish at 5 p.m. I was on my way to the supermarket to pick up some things. As I left my driveway, I was traveling southeast, and I saw something in the sky. At first, I thought it was a blimp. I was so excited because I hadn't seen a blimp since I was six years old, and I just wanted to see what company was advertising on this blimp.

In Australia at the time, there was such a hard lockdown from Covid that we couldn't cross states. The closest airport to my house maybe had two flights a day. So there was barely ever anything in the skies. So when I saw this thing, it was exciting. I said to myself, "Oh my God, it's a blimp! So cool!"

I was traveling southeast, and I was driving towards a highway, and I noticed the blimp in the sky was getting lower. It wasn't moving in a forward or left/right trajectory. It was just descending. So I don't actually know how blimps move. I don't even know if that is possible. But that was what I was seeing. As I was getting closer to the highway, I was almost directly underneath this blimp. But that was when I realized it wasn't a blimp.

This object was a triangular shape. It had no distinct wings. I would say it was probably about ten stories up. It was quite large, about the size of a 747. It had three lights on each point. They were round and a bluish white color.

I was freaking out at this point. My mind was going a million miles an hour. I was still driving at this stage, and I noticed that this thing was not traveling. It was at a complete standstill above the highway, pointing south towards Byron Bay. It was about 5:10 p.m., and this highway was bumper-to-bumper traffic, so I was thinking, "Oh my God... everyone's seeing this!"

I tried calling my partner on the Bluetooth in my car. I knew that this thing was too low for him to see from our house, but I was still trying to call him, telling him to get outside and look up. As I was calling, I was now directly underneath this thing. And the thing that really freaked me out was that there was no sound coming from it. Nothing.

I couldn't remain stopped though because I was literally on the highway in traffic, so I took my exit and crossed over the highway. I looked back in my rearview mirror, and this thing was gone! I didn't see it take off. Nothing. I was thinking, *How did that thing disappear like that? Surely I would have heard a boom or something for it just to shoot off like that!*

Once I got off the exit, I went to the parking lot of the supermarket, and I tried calling my sister, and she didn't answer. I just wanted to tell someone what I'd just seen. I texted her about it, and then that was it. Between her and my partner, those were the only two people that I ever told. I didn't think anyone would believe me. But since then, I've been able to share my story with work friends and other close friends. And everyone actually did believe me.

So for months after, I was searching the news and social media, thinking someone would have reported this. Someone would have seen exactly what I saw. It was such a busy day on the highway, and this thing was so low. But nothing. I've never heard anyone report it.

So after that, it kind of sparked my interest in UFOs. And then I was listening to the *Somewhere in the Skies* podcast, and there was a *Witness Accounts* episode all about people who'd seen triangular UFOs. I was like, "Yes! That's what I saw!"

It was an absolutely crazy experience. Now I am fully involved in the topic. I love listening to the podcast and reading books and watching documentaries on UFOs.

More than anything, I constantly look up now. In hopes to see the next one.

ON THE BEACHES OF EL SALVADOR

My name is Osvaldo Castillo. I currently reside in Vancouver, Canada. I have two sightings to share. The first one happened in 2005 when I was visiting my family in El Salvador. That's where I'm from. And in the months of June and July, I was visiting my family. And at some point in the month of July, I had rented out a hut. It was a very rustic place by the beach. This portion of the beach is along the coastline that's isolated from any sort of development or tourism. It's mostly populated by local fishermen and their families.

Back in 2005, on my second night there, I had gotten into the habit of pulling a chair out from my hut and dragging it over to the beach when the tide was out, usually around 8 or 9 p.m. I got into stargazing mode, which was so much fun because it was such a beautiful place.

This night was a starry night. No cloud cover whatsoever. I was just really serenely looking up at the sky into the horizon. It was really dark by then. All of a sudden, I saw this light start to intensify. As it became brighter really quickly, it started to shoot down as if it was going to crash into the ocean. Then, out of nowhere, it made this forty-five-degree angle upward, and as it did that, it made this flash of lightning. Kind of like in *Star Trek* when the ships go into warp speed, and they create this lightning at the end. That's the closest I can describe what I saw.

The whole thing lasted for three or four seconds. It had this accelerated movement to it. This is, again, 2005. Unfortunately, it's a poor country, and El Salvador's military didn't have anything like the drone technology of today. I don't even know if commercial drone use was around back then. But the movement this light made... it was just crazy fast.

It was not a meteorite. This thing did not burn up, because it started to shoot down in a very irregular manner. Like it had this irregular, jerky movement, but really quick. It just showed up, and it did this flash of lightning. That's definitely not a meteorite. I also don't think it was a satellite, a plane, or a fisherman's boat. Those can all be discounted, in my opinion. I don't know what the hell it was. But I was just astounded. If anything, it felt like it was something out of this world.

I just went to bed that night with the knowledge that I had seen something really amazing. And I put this experience on the shelf for the longest time, because as soon as it happened, I looked around me, and there were no other witnesses. It was just me on that beach. And sure, I could have shared it with my family, but I chose not to back then, on account of El Salvador being a very Christian country, and they would have taken my story and just placed it in the "looney bin" and probably would have asked what I was smoking that night! But let me tell you, though, my mind was totally lucid that night. I was in my state of mind.

Before this incident, I was open to the topic of UFOs, but I was never really someone who would go out and investigate it or really get into it. So again, I put this story in the back of my mind for the longest time. Until my second sighting that occurred in Canada, in 2021.

I now live in Vancouver. This happened in May of 2021 around midnight. My apartment is in this block building, and I'm on the third floor. My roommates and I have this bulky balcony that's south facing, and in front of us, there's a parking lot. There are these really beautiful, tall maple trees that shoot up about 180 to 200 feet high. Then there's a row of about six or seven pine trees next to them.

I'm in my living room, and all of a sudden there's a power outage. I think to myself, *We haven't had one of those in a while.* And the thing about me is that I'm a night owl. I stay up really late. So I end up stepping outside to once again gaze up at the sky. And when I do so, I look to my left and right, and both rows of houses next to our building... their lights are out, too. Then I look up into the sky, and I see these three dots of light. They were white and yellow. And these three were in a triangle formation, just gliding across, going southeast. Just gliding silently. I was just mesmerized by this triangle UFO.

It was hard to tell how big and how high the lights were, but I do know that that they went over those tall maple trees. And as they were moving southeast, they disappeared out of sight.

I remember just being really spooked because it was just the sequence of events in which this happened. Was this coincidence or synchronicity? Was this thing what caused the power outage in our building and for the rest of the row of houses next to our building? I still ask myself that. As it happened, I remember I was really scared standing on that balcony. But I also wanted to communicate with it. I wanted to say to it, "Stay. I want to keep seeing more."

The next day, I just had to tell my partner about it. I also reported it to MUFON (Mutual UFO Network) and other places. But overall, I think the first sighting was just astounding. The second one... there was something palpable there and how it made me feel. I think this topic really challenges the status quo of what we currently understand about the cosmos and ourselves as human beings. I'm not saying that the sightings that I had were of alien origin, but the first one was truly something out of this world. It was something that I had never seen.

I have this uncanny feeling that it'll keep happening. That I'm going to keep seeing or having more UFO experiences or sightings. I can't tell you why that is, but I know it's going to happen. I just don't know when. And that's okay.

I just know that I have to keep looking up.

BETWEEN EDINBURGH AND GLASGOW

My name is John Brown. I live in a small, semi-rural village in southern Scotland. I worked full-time as a corrections officer for over fourteen years. My experience happened on October 22, 2017, which was just before that now-famous *New York Times* article released about UFOs and the Pentagon.

It was roughly 9 p.m. at night, and I had been in my garage, which I used as sort of a man-cave type area, where I'd do hobbies and such. I was closing up at night, and I was heading back up to the house, collecting a few items to take up with me that I didn't want to leave in the garage all night. Ironically, I actually included my Nikon DSLR slung over my shoulder at the time.

So I pulled down the garage door and walked up the driveway towards the house. I had a quick look at my phone, and then I looked up. My attention was drawn to what I could only describe as two warm, white lights sitting right next to one another, moving in a figure-eight pattern, if it were on its side. I could only describe these things as traveling at breakneck speed, really moving across the sky.

The whole encounter only lasted a short amount of time. A

few seconds probably. They were moving at a low altitude, so it drew my attention right away. We were somewhat close to an Air Force base called RAF Lossiemouth. It still has jets stationed there, so I've seen lots of low-flying fighter jets. This was nothing like that. It was moving, but there was no sound. It was a straight trajectory, it wasn't arced, so it was flying level. The forward of the two lights was pulsating. The other light was solid the entire time. But then, as it moved across, from my perspective, it was going from the right to the left. The pulsating light then very quickly faded, and I never saw it again.

We're roughly halfway between Glasgow and Edinburgh, probably slightly closer to Glasgow. And both of those cities have airports, so we have craft fly over the house all the time. Normally, at that height, you will hear the aircraft engines pretty loud, but they're usually substantially higher in the sky than this object was. But it was silent. Eerily silent. It was a quiet and clear night.

After the lights disappeared, I stood for a few minutes and tried to gather my thoughts, wondering what it was I had just witnessed. I considered all sorts of possibilities: aircraft or helicopters, possibly. It was also close to the fifth of November when people celebrate Guy Fawkes Night, so there's usually lots of fireworks and stuff going on. But this was not fireworks. There was no sound and no contrails.

There was a road nearby, so I considered that maybe it could have been car lights. But in the direction it was heading, it would have to be heading up the hill, in which case you would see the red taillights of the car, as opposed to the white lights. I considered the possibility of a drone, as well. But again, the speed was absolutely incredible.

It was a strange experience. I think about it most days, usually when I'm popping into the garage to do a couple of jobs. I always look up at that same spot and think back to that night, and it still stumps me as to what it was. I'm not saying this is little green men from Mars or trans-dimensional entities or anything like that. But I can't explain what this is. It really made me feel strange. I mentioned that I had my camera slung over my shoulder. I also had my mobile phone in my hand. But the thought never occurred to me to take a photograph. I was just transfixed on this object. I don't even think I would have had enough time to get a shot off.

This was by far one of the more strange experiences of my entire life. I still think about it to this day and wonder, what was it that I saw in the sky that night?

A DIAMOND IN THE SKY

My name is Larry Gessner, and I live in McClusky, North Dakota. I spent over fourteen years in the United States Air Force, working my way up from a weapons technician bomb loader to master instructor, teaching the entire weapons system on the B-52 bomber to fighter pilots and other technicians. After the military, I spent the next eight years on the police force, eventually retiring as sheriff in Sheridan County.

The event that I'm going to talk about happened to me and my wife on July 7, 2003. I had just gotten home, and I had sat down in the living room to watch television. Had to be about 11 p.m. or so. My wife decided she wanted to go outside on the back deck to smoke a cigarette. So I was watching one of the late night shows, and all of a sudden, my wife started screaming. I immediately jumped into law enforcement mode, thinking someone was trying to hurt her, so I raced out the back door to find her on the deck, pointing up in the sky.

She then proceeded to tell me that one of the stars shot out of the sky, it stopped, and these red lights came on. So I looked up, and at first, I thought it was probably a meteor or something. But then I was looking at these red lights above the horizon, and it looked like they were off in the distance. But not too far. And all of a sudden, I was thinking to myself, *It almost looks like that thing is headed towards us! A*nd then as it started to get closer, I thought maybe it was an aircraft or something that we just didn't understand what it was. But as the object started to get closer, I noticed that there were now green lights as well. And the lights were all in a vertical formation.

It just really puzzled me because I've been around aircraft my whole life. And I knew the light configuration of aircraft. And when I looked up at this thing, I just knew that something was not right. As it got closer, we could tell it was farther up in the sky. We estimated maybe it was around eight hundred feet in the sky. And it was big. The best way I can describe it would be to compare it to the size of an American football field. About one hundred yards long and around fifty yards wide.

So this thing was starting to come closer, and I saw a white light up in the corner of it. And then we started to hear what I automatically assumed was the sound of thrust from an aircraft. But the object was traveling so slow. Probably around thirty miles per hour or something like that. Then, all of a sudden, I realized that this side light was a window. And it was backlit from the inside of what appeared to be some sort of craft. And the craft was starting to take on what I would characterize as a diamond shape.

As it was getting closer, we were looking up at it, and I heard this thrust sound. But the thrust sound did not equate to what I knew thrust to be from jet engines on an aircraft. There wasn't enough of the sound of thrust to keep a thing of this size up in the air. So I was just totally bewildered.

It finally got to just about over our heads, and I was freaking out. My wife was freaking out. We were looking at this thing, and I was trying to focus on the window at this point. There were two sets or two rows of windows, and I was focused probably on the upper set. And I could see inside the window. So I started thinking to myself, *Am I about to see an alien?!*

What I did see was some sort of a structural wall. Now in aircraft design, they drill out holes in support structures to lessen oblique. This is an engineering thing that they do. I've seen this before in the structural integrity of the B-52s. So I was looking at this, and I was saying to myself, "My God... this thing is man-made!"

At this point my wife and I were just dumbfounded. I mean, you become paralyzed because your brain is trying to make sense of something that isn't making any sense to you. This was, by all means, a UFO.

At this point, it started to head southeast just behind our house. And as it was overhead, I realize it was heading right for an area where one of my deputies lived. So I ran inside to call my deputy while my wife stayed outside and followed the object, and my wife ran to the side of the house to follow the object. My deputy answered the phone, and I told him, "You've got to get outside right now... there's a UFO headed right over your house!"

He was laughing at me on the phone, and I proceeded to tell him, "I'm dead serious. Get outside!" So he finally got outside. And about that same time, I ran out the front door to see where the object was, and I just saw my wife standing there. She told me, "You're not gonna believe this, but as soon as you said the word UFO, the craft stopped dead, a white light came out the back end of it, and it shot straight up in the air, and it was gone!"

At that point, we knew we had seen something incredible. Something that either we have the capability to have ships like that, or we are being visited by an intelligent race. The craft was of an unbelievable size. I honestly don't know what this craft would have been used for. And the thing that I'm still trying to wrap my head around is when they travel those unbelievable speeds and stop, how is it that they can do that? If you're driving in a car and you slam on the brakes, you launch forward! So when you're traveling at, let's say, a thousand miles an hour... I just can't imagine how anybody could survive something like that without breaking the laws of physics.

In 2019, my story caught the attention of Luis Elizondo. Elizondo was the former head of AATIP, the Pentagon's once secret UFO program. I agreed to speak with Elizondo for the History Channel television series *Unidentified: Inside America's UFO Investigation*. In the episode, I brought Elizondo to the exact location where the sighting had occurred. I was excited not only to meet Elizondo in person, but to tell my story on a scale I never thought I'd be able to.

After sharing the sighting with him, he sprang something on me that every UFO witness hopes to hear, but rarely ever does. He told me that someone else had seen what I had seen!

I was stunned. He didn't elaborate, and I didn't ask for any more information. This floored me at first because no one else had come forward that I was aware of. And even though Elizondo wouldn't divulge who this other witness was, I did recall one other witness who had previously come forward to me, personally. This was in confidence that it would not be made public. They claimed that they'd seen this diamond-shaped object shoot straight up and out of sight. It was actually his father who told me this. So the only way that information could have reached Elizondo would have been if it was shared via phone conversation and intercepted through someone listening.

This left me wondering, could AATIP have actually been looking into this incident long before this television program? But even more interesting was a conversation I had with Elizondo before he left. He proposed that the location where I had the sighting was in close proximity to Minot Air Force Base and several nuclear installations. Knowing that missile silos were disabled during UFO events, and seeing that these were in the path of this craft I'd witnessed, it gave Elizondo concern.

Was what I saw a top-secret military craft? I remain open to the possibility, but also can't deny that the craft's structure, maneuvers, and acceleration remained much more advanced than anything I'd ever imagined from US technology. Knowing that the craft stopped and shot straight up at the moment that I said UFO to my deputy on the phone always made me think that whoever was on that thing had caught that conversation. For me, that will always be more than a coincidence. I think Elizondo was letting me know that the US government is capable of tracking them. It is probably still classified, and that is why he did not say any more about it.

Having now met a former member of a highly secretive Pentagon UFO program, I felt more vindicated than ever. I really enjoyed the conversations I had with Elizondo during the time he was here. I genuinely believe that he took his job at AATIP very seriously and continues to dedicate himself to finding the answers to help provide not only the proof, but help us provide a defense if they turn out to be a positive threat.

I have always been a levelheaded guy, and I would not say I saw something unless I saw it. I look forward to a time when memories can be shown somehow, and then others can see what I have seen. I want to believe that before I pass from this world, I'll get the full story of that craft and what it was doing.

Let's find out what they *all* are doing.

THE KENTUCKY PASTURE AFFAIR

My name is Bill McCray. I currently reside in Central Florida. At the time of this sighting, I was living in my hometown in Northern Kentucky back in the early 1980s. Myself, my dad who has since passed, and several of my friends were standing out in the front yard of my grandparents' house. When this happened, I was staying with my grandparents.

We were overlooking this pasture that butted up to the property that my grandparents had in the housing development where they lived. Several of us were standing there, and we looked over into the pasture, which was part of a big ranch owned by a well-known family in my hometown. We looked, and there was something floating across the sky, shining a light down on the pasture. When we first saw it, it had to be a quarter mile away. But then it continued to come towards us. When it finally got the closest it was going to be, it was approximately two hundred feet away and about a hundred and fifty feet in the air. No noise whatsoever. If it had been a helicopter shining down the light, we obviously would have heard it. The other reason I don't believe it was a helicopter was because the lights from the big barn on the ranch kind of backlit the object itself.

The object was approximately thirty feet across. It was flat on the bottom, and the light was coming out at the bottom. It was somewhat dome shaped on the top. Well... maybe a combination of dome-shaped and slightly triangular or pyramid-shaped across the top. It's kind of hard to describe, but that's the best way I can describe it: a combination of the top part of the dome with slight triangular features.

This craft continued to shine the light down in various places in the pasture itself. Quite often, the family's herd of cows would be out in this pasture, using it as grazing land. I don't believe there were any cows out there at the time.

It was not making a sound, and it was getting closer. It stopped about two hundred feet from us, and it was still shining this light down on the pasture. This whole sighting probably took a good three to four minutes from the time that we saw it first shine the light down about a quarter mile away until it got to the closest that it actually was. After this, it started heading off back towards the edge of the property of the ranch in the opposite direction of where we were. We were all standing there transfixed. And eventually, it just ended up going over a hill, continually shining this light down. It eventually went over this hill and out of sight.

After all was said and done, we all just stood there. In Northern Kentucky, it's not unusual to have sightings of unidentified objects in the air. It's not quite commonplace, but it's enough to where it doesn't surprise folks when we get reports of unidentified objects or things of that nature. So we weren't shocked by it. But we were all scratching our heads, trying to figure out what it was. To this day I still have no idea.

Being a person who is interested in sightings of this nature, I looked for potential articles in the hometown newspaper of cattle mutilations and things like that after the sighting. Nothing. But I do know what I saw. Unfortunately, I can't ask my dad anything else about it since he's no longer with us.

While I wasn't afraid of what I saw, it left me with a sense of wonder. Not every question in the world has been answered, and we still have things we need to figure out.

BATTLE OVER THE ROCKY MOUNTAINS

My name is Cameron Brauer. I grew up in northern Montana right near the Canadian border. The nearest town, with over a hundred people in it, was about twenty-five miles away. So I was surrounded by acres of empty prairie and an endless sky full of stars. And in this part of Montana, you can definitely see some UFOs. I would almost guarantee that if anyone went out to that part of the prairie, only a mile or so from the house that I grew up in, and spent three or so nights looking, you'd probably see a UFO.

My friends and I spent countless nights sleeping under the stars there. We'd see amazing things like shooting stars and satellites. We'd see other things that looked like satellites, but probably weren't. And in the summer of 1983, I saw something that definitely was not a satellite.

It was the summer between my sophomore and junior year of high school. I had a job at a radio station. My usual shift was about 6 p.m. to midnight. I would drive about twenty-five miles to and from work several times a week. That always gave me a chance to do a lot of thinking and also to look for lights in the sky.

So one night I was traveling home a little later than usual. I was the only car on the road. This was not unusual. If you were on this stretch of highway, you were most likely a trucker going to or coming from Canada. So I was halfway home and listening to my AM radio in my old '66 Chevy, when all of a sudden an emerald green light lit up the whole sky. I'm talking the entire sky. The light was coming from my side of the car, and I quickly looked over just in time to see a green streak of something cross the horizon. There was also a *whoosh* sound. But not so much because of the object, but it was almost like the object made its own sound. I know that's hard to understand, but there was definitely a *whoosh* sound. I estimate the light was more than forty miles away but less than eighty miles away.

I could see the Rocky Mountains behind the light, and I saw something else as well. I saw what looked like dozens of dots and dashes that were peppering the night sky just above the horizon of the Rockies. I knew these dots were the profiles of some kind of craft that were probably floating in the night sky. They were absolutely in formation, and I could barely make them out after the green light was totally gone. But they remained there maybe for twenty seconds or more, just kind of hovering. Then something incredible happened.

In formation, the dots moved slightly forward and then made an abrupt ascent and began spiraling in formation into the sky. They were in groups, spiraling and heading vertical. Then, there was a flash of green at the highest point in their travel, and they became one green streak that actually glowed a little greener in the sky as they continued straight up. They definitely seemed to bleed into one streak as they stretched up and out of sight in an incredible flash and an incredible demonstration of speed. And in less than a second, they were gone.

I didn't get the impression they were making that green glow at all. I'm thinking they were under fire or trying to make an escape. I couldn't see anything pursuing them, but for sure they were trying to flee something.

I can't help but wonder if I witnessed some kind of interstellar battle right here in the middle of Montana skies.

A FAMILY LEFT BEAMING

My name is Vince Bucy. I live in Brunswick, Ohio, which is just right outside of Cleveland. I had just moved into a new house, and our old house was less than a mile away. My routine was that I would work my nine-to-five job, and after, I'd spend time with the family and eat dinner. I would get ready to go work on the old house to get it ready to sell.

One night, I finished up around 1 a.m. On the way home, I was going through my development. That was when I saw something in the sky. It was visually probably about two inches above the tree line. It was strange enough that I stopped and got out of my car to take a look at it. I can admit that I was pretty tired at the time. I looked at it, and I was going to just shrug it off. But I was about a thousand feet from my driveway, so I drove on. I got in my driveway, got out, and took another good look at it. And I just knew something wasn't right.

First of all, in the night sky, it was slightly larger than my thumb. I wouldn't say that it was giving off light. I would say that it was illuminated. It looked like the moon would, low on the horizon, on a hazy, humid dark night. But this was definitely not the moon. It was just an eerie white.

I stood there, and I watched it. And then I thought to myself, *No one is gonna believe this...*

So I ran into the house. This was a school night, and it was almost 2 a.m. at this point. I woke my daughter and my son up. My daughter was sixteen, and my son was thirteen. I got them to come outside. My son, being the skeptic that he is, probably lasted about three minutes, taking a look at it, and said, "I'm going inside." But, being his dad, I knew that he went inside because he was scared. You could see the fear in his eyes.

My daughter and I stayed out in the driveway and watched it a couple more minutes. Then I realized I had binoculars inside, and I knew exactly where they were because I'd done all the boxing when we moved out of the old house. So I went inside and got the binoculars and ran back outside.

I took the first view through the binoculars, and I couldn't believe what I was looking at. I was looking at something that was egg-shaped. The best way I can describe it is that the bottom of it looked like it was made out of old clad-iron rivets, like you'd see on an old ship or an old submarine with seams. But it just looked old. And from the halfway point up, it looked really modern. I remember vividly seeing what looked like louvers, like you'd see on an old, old muscle car.

This is going to sound crazy, but I also remember that the top of it was shaped like a genie's lamp. That's the best way I could describe this thing.

I gave the binoculars to my daughter, and she described it very similar to how I did. We watched it for about another five minutes, trading off the binoculars, and this thing was not moving. It was just in the sky, and it was not moving at all. I looked at it through the binoculars one more time, and it scared me to death. Something had changed.

It looked like it was sitting on top of a pedestal. A gray and white pedestal of some sort. It had rigid edges.

I handed the binoculars to my daughter, and I asked her to tell me what had changed. I didn't want to tell her what I had seen. She looked at it, and she looked at me, and she said, "Oh my God... there's a beam of light coming out of it!"

At this point, we both were freaked out. She lasted probably about another two or three minutes, and she was scared to death. She ran inside. I, on the other hand, stood out there for about another two to three minutes. And then I started to feel that fear they'd both felt as well. I felt like I was seeing something that I was not supposed to see. And ironically enough, that's how my daughter explained it to me later on.

I finally went inside, and I was exhausted. I took a shower, and then I went to bed. Once in bed, I realized I could see this thing. It was right outside my bedroom window! That was when I noticed this thing actually was moving. It was moving so slow that the only way I could tell was by the frame of my window. I watched it in comparison, and it was moving so slow, like you would see the moon move if you were sky-watching. It was moving horizontally, though, and I watched it for at least another fifteen minutes until it disappeared, and I finally, somehow, went to sleep.

The next morning, I decided I was going to make a call to the Mutual UFO Network (MUFON). It must have been a pretty good story, because within twenty-four hours, I had a field investigator at my doorstep. It was really nice to have someone to tell my story to, and he did a great job of showing me, with his program, what was supposed to be in the night sky and what shouldn't be in the night sky. And what I saw that night was *not* supposed to be there.

This experience was both amazing and terrifying. But I cannot wait to hopefully see something like this again.

THE SKIES OF MONSTERLAND

My name is Ronny Le Blanc. I co-host the television series *Expedition Bigfoot* and authored the book *Monsterland: Encounters with UFOs, Bigfoot and Orange Orbs.* The event I want to share with you happened on June 5, 2021.

At approximately 9:30 p.m., my wife and I were in our garage, talking. We walked out and were heading inside our house. I happened to look up above the roof of the house. That was when I saw two unmistakable UFOs. One was red, and one was green. Not like flying saucers, but almost like orbs that were shape-shifting and changing. What stuck out was that these things were chasing each other in the sky, up and down, almost like dolphins in the water. While this was happening, my wife was trying to get her phone out. Although, I didn't want to film this at all. I was just experiencing it.

These were not drones. They were not planes. These were straight-up UFOs. I started feeling euphoric. Super excited to be watching this because I knew this was something extraordinary!

I live really close to Leominster State Forest in Massachusetts.

To locals, it's also known as "Monsterland," which is what my book was based on. There's a lot of strange activity in this area.

So I started to talk to my wife about where these objects had possibly come from, direction-wise. And sure enough, as we were talking about this, another one came! This one was like this bluish kind of green. It was silent like the others. Only this one was sort of spinning and changing shape. It followed the trajectory of the others, beyond some trees.

My wife finally got her camera up, and we were looking in the path of these things, waiting for another one to come. And I could feel like it was coming, which sounds crazy, I know. But here it came. This time, it was green, and it actually flew right over our heads!

The crazy thing is, a minute or so before these sightings occurred, as we were sitting in our garage, my wife was touched three times on her leg. Like a ghost or something. She felt like something was in the garage with us. I just kind of chuckled and laughed. And we were sitting close to each other, just laughing about it. But this happened three times. And then we saw these four UFOs, one after another, at the same time. We were blown away. One of the most amazing things, if not the most amazing thing I've ever seen in my life.

We just stood outside. My head was spinning, and my energy was off the charts. My ten-year-old son was inside, and he came out and told us that he could hear us talking outside about the UFO. And as he heard us, he felt some sort of presence behind him, inside. I found that aspect about this extremely significant.

Another significant, yet funny occurrence was that my wife went grocery shopping and picked up a deck of cards. And as I was grabbing the trash that day, one of these cards in this deck came out, and it was called "stargazer." Just kind of funny. I always look at signs and synchronicities, and this is just one of those things.

I don't believe that what I saw that day were physical craft. It just seemed to shape-shift and change. It almost seemed more biological. It moved like a bird. It seemed to float and flutter and kind of change direction and move very animalistically.

Recently, I've gotten back into meditating. I'm focusing on remote viewing. So earlier that day, I did have a short five-minute meditation session. And I kid you not, I was trying to bring in UFOs. I've done this before a couple of years ago at Cape Cod here in Massachusetts. I actually had these orange orbs come in. But I've never had craft or large objects like what we saw that night.

I do believe there's a spiritual and a paranormal kind of connection to all of this. Especially because of what happened prior to this UFO sighting. That feeling of a presence. Not only for my wife, but my son as well.

There was a report that someone saw something a couple of weeks prior to this event, in the same vicinity. And their sighting occurred right in front of the Big Dipper, which was exactly where our sighting took place in the sky as well. I find all of this very interesting.

There's definitely something strange going on in and above Monsterland.

THERE BE DRAGONS

My name is Brandon Sturgill. I don't typically share these stories with anybody. Only people whom I trust and who I know will believe me.

The first event happened back in the summer of 2003. I was in the Northern Neck region of Virginia towards the coast. It's a very agricultural rural area. A lot of woodland, too. My friend Jenn and I had been out there visiting a mutual friend, and we were on our way back to her parents' house in Southern Maryland, where we were staying for the night.

We were driving along a two-lane road, and it was very dark. It was like a black canvas in the sky. There weren't any streetlights either. Just thick woods on both sides of the road. So we were riding along, and I was in the passenger seat. I looked down to pick out a CD, and as I was doing so, I saw this very intense blue light come pouring in through the windshield. I immediately looked up. The blue light filled the entire car. I looked to my left, above the tree line, and I saw this brilliant bright light that was oblong shaped. Like a football. The color was like a royal blue. It was glowing intensely.

I thought to myself something that Jenn almost simultaneously said aloud... "What is that?"

This thing went from a stationary position in the sky to just basically gone in like the snap of a finger. I saw this blue streak take off, which was pretty much parallel with the road we were traveling on. It just shot straight ahead in the same direction we were going, at lightning speed.

Jenn was very shaken by it. For our safety, I encouraged her to pull over and let me drive the rest of the way home. I wanted to talk about what just happened, but Jenn actually had the idea that we wait until we get back to her parents' house and separately draw what we saw and compare the two and see if we think we saw the same thing.

We said maybe five words the rest of the ride to Southern Maryland. When we got to her parents' house, she first sat at the kitchen table and drew what she saw. I sat in the living room and tried to distract myself and calm myself down. A little while later, I went in to the kitchen and drew what I saw. Then we compared the two.

We had drawn the exact same shape. We used the same colors, and we drew it in the same position above the tree line to our left. It was a mirror image. We felt like this added another layer of validity to the fact that it was something tangible. It was something that was truly there in the sky in that moment, and it looked and behaved like nothing we had seen before.

I had always been a believer. I understood the fact that this universe is infinite, and who are we to say there is not an abundant amount of life out there. Whether it be in our own reality or our own universe. Or whether it's coming from some sort of other dimension. I have no clue. But I went into that experience already believing it's fairly likely. But seeing what we saw that night... it reinforced the idea that the things that people claim to see... a lot of them are probably telling the truth. Of course, a bunch of them are probably making it up and wanting attention. But I experienced it too. I became one of those people.

The second sighting happened sixteen years later in the fall of 2019. I stopped at a gas station in Roanoke, Virginia, where I was living at the time. It was a beautiful day. Blue skies. No clouds. It was about 5 p.m., so it was too early for stars to be plentiful in the sky. I ran into the gas station real quick, and when I came back out, I happened to look up to my right, and I saw this round, solid white object in the sky.

It was literally the only thing in the sky. My first thought was that maybe it was a plane or a drone or something like that. But it made no noise. And in a similar circumstance to the first encounter, there was no sense of scale to apply. It was just a blue sky with nothing else around it. So I thought, *If it's a plane, then I'll stand here and watch it from the same perspective for a couple of minutes. If it gets larger or smaller, then I can assume it's a plane either coming in my direction or going away.* It didn't travel at all. It was just hanging there.

After a couple of minutes, it started erratically moving around the sky at varying speeds. It went left-right, up-down, diagonal at slower speeds and at very quick speeds. It was like it was just teleporting to different parts of the sky.

I was by myself in that moment, watching it and just flabbergasted, trying to figure out what it was. It wasn't making any noise either. Then I noticed that there were about a dozen other people in the parking lot looking up at the same thing. And while it was bouncing around the sky, we were all just standing there, bewildered by what we were seeing. We all ended up congregating together in the middle of the parking lot and watching it together for probably fifteen minutes. I was actually the last to watch it until it vanished. I couldn't tell where it went. It just vanished.

I can't even begin to explain how it was moving the way that it moved. Very erratic aerial vehicles that we've designed, at this point in our history, can't move that way.

I did take some video of it, but unfortunately, the video is not very compelling because with it being a solid blue sky, I'm moving my phone around to keep it in frame. You're basically just seeing blue everywhere it goes. In the video, it just looks like an object that's staying completely still against this blue sky. But it was actually moving all over the place.

These two experiences reinforced my opinion that there's something out there that we can't explain. Or at least, that the public is not aware of and able to explain. It doesn't scare me, though. It excites me. It gets my mind going as to what it could be. And those possibilities are endless. But it's apparent when you experience something like that, like so many have, that you can't even begin to explain it, that you don't know how to put it into a perspective that fits your known reality; it's just something crazy. Like if a dragon came flying down out of the air and flew overhead! It's just something that doesn't fit our reality and what we know of existence. And to me, that's very exciting.

I hope, in my lifetime, I'll get more answers.

THE HELLFIRE CLUB

My name is Ben O'Neill, and I'm from Ireland. I've had a number of weird encounters and sightings since I was a kid. I live at the foot of Montpelier Hill in Dublin, where you can look up the hill and you can see the old ruins of a building where, in the 1700s, the Irish Hellfire Club called home. However, after numerous reports of paranormal activity and haunted goings-on, the group relocated away from the lodge, and it was left abandoned.

To my north is Casement Aerodrome, an airbase. So we're basically in the flight path of the Air Corps, passenger jets, helicopters, and the Coast Guard.

So it was April of 2021. The family was all in the house, where we had a family event. And I ended up getting volunteered to go to the shop. So I put my headphones in and started walking. I was going through the estate we were in, and I looked up. There was this plane, and I could hear it through my headphones. So I took my headphones out, and I realized this plane was really low over the estate. Too low. And it was turning. Not banking so much, but trying to turn to its right. So I was watching it fly over and fly off.

And I just found it weird. I could see the flight path it was taking, and it was going towards this red star off in the distance.

This was a really bright red star. It was quite low down on the horizon, and I just kept watching. I was walking through the estate, and it was just weird to me because it was still fairly bright out. It wasn't night yet, but there was this bright, red star there. So I kept watching the plane flying towards the red star.

At this point, I made it to the shop. I went in and grabbed my stuff. And as I was walking out and started heading to the estates, I was looking for that red star again. And it was gone. So I just started walking home. And I got to my driveway, and I was glancing at the mountain, and I was glancing back at the spot where that star was. And when I looked at the mountain itself, there were these two white lights over it. I was watching these two lights, and they were finding each other, side by side, and they went up, and they just moved over and back again. I thought maybe they were some sort of lights in the trees on the mountain, but then they started moving above the tree line.

At the time, I thought it was maybe two drones flying together. But it just doesn't really make a ton of sense to me when I consider the other things that happened almost eight months later.

So it was early December. I was coming back home at about midnight. I was walking through the estates, and as I was walking, I looked over at the mountain, and there were those two white lights again! Only this time, as I was watching, I noticed there were more of them. There were three different objects, each with these pairs of lights. One of them had a little flashing red light in the middle that kind of flashed in weird intervals.

This was happening right over the Hellfire Club. And it looked like they were scanning the mountain. I kept watching them as they moved off; they moved together. Then, all of sudden, they all came to the center, over a random spot over the forest, and they just kind of slowly drifted off. One went right. One went left. And one actually went over the mountain and disappeared.

So I was watching this all play out, and then I just turned around and went into the house. And that reaction or response to the experience still confuses me to this day. Sometimes you hear that people who see these things, sometimes they're like, "Oh, I just turned away, and I went to sleep," or something like that. It's weird. For me, I didn't even think, *I should record this!* And I didn't even bother to watch where the lights went after they went in different directions. I just turned around and went inside. It makes no sense.

So maybe three weeks afterwards, my friends and I were walking through a nearby park, trying to meet up with other friends before Christmas to give each other gifts. And it was kind of late. Pitch black outside at this point. We were going through the park, and I was telling my friends about the lights that I saw. I was describing the one with the middle flashing red light. And as I was describing it, right above us, we all looked up, and it was literally above us!

I told my friends that was exactly what had been over the mountain. And they were all kind of glancing up, and they were all like, "Yeah, yeah. It looks like a drone." And then they all just moved. And these are people who've had experiences themselves in the area. And this was happening right in front of them, and they just lost interest. Exactly the same way that I had when I had been at the door of my house. They just turned away and started talking amongst themselves. It actually really freaked me out. So did the odds of me talking about that thing and then it just spontaneously appears directly above us. That's one hell of a coincidence!

Those are my sightings. I don't really know how I feel about any of them, honestly. I'm a little bit freaked out more than I am anything else. I've never experienced that feeling of just losing interest in something so quickly as it's happening. And then for it to happen at the exact moment I'm describing it to friends. It was all just so bizarre to me.

I really don't know how to explain what happened, and what continues to happen, over the Hellfire Club.

ALONE ON THE PLAYGROUND

My name is Kyle Newman, and I am from Oregon. This story happened to me in the fourth grade. I'm now thirty-three, so this was quite some time ago. At the time, my mom would drive both me and my older brother up to school. He was in middle school, and I was in elementary school. His classes generally started quite a bit earlier than mine. So we would drop him off at school and take a short trip down the road to the elementary school, where my mom and I would sit in the car and wait. Usually, she'd read to me. I specifically remember, at this time, her reading me one of the *Animorphs* books, which was huge back then.

On this particular day, I looked out the window of the car and realized that nobody was there yet, and I could have the entire playground to myself. So after some coaxing, my mom finally let me go play by myself on the empty playground. Knowing that people would be showing up any minute, my mom left.

So I'm playing for a bit, and then I noticed this big rectangular object passing over the school. It was so low that it looked like it wasn't even going to clear the building. Even as a fourth-grader, I could have tossed a rock up and hit it!

I was transfixed on this thing. I had no idea, in my little brain, what it could have been. I didn't see it from the side, at least not to my recollection, but I remember seeing the back. It was pretty big. As big, if not just a little bit bigger than the school was. I just stared at this thing until it cleared the building and I couldn't see it anymore. And then it hit me.

I ran to the swing set on the playground and started to swing. I wanted to see if I could swing high enough to still see it. I started pumping my little legs as hard as I could to see if I could see where this thing went, where it was going, or even if it was still there.

I told my brother about this sighting after it happened, and he dismissed it outright. And recently, he asked me why I was so interested in all this UFO stuff. And I reminded him of this sighting. Told him the whole story again. And all he said was, "That was so long ago. You're probably misremembering a lot of that. The human memory is fickle." And while I give him that, there's just some things that are so important... big moments in your life that you tend to remember very vividly. This event was one of those moments.

I'm never going to forget it. It's always going to be there.

Crystal clear.

THE BRONX INVASION

My name is Miguel Rodriguez. I'm a native New Yorker, born and raised in the Bronx. I currently live in South Florida, where I work for the Broward County School Board. I have two sightings I want to share. One as a child and one as an adult.

My initial sighting took place in 1989. I was twelve years old. The building that I lived in, from my bedroom, I could see the Manhattan skyline and all of Queens. Directly in front of me was the Hudson River and the Whitestone Bridge.

On this particular night, I saw what appeared to be a luminescent orb over the bridge. This orb was pulsating brilliantly. It almost looked like a mini moon. It was rocking back and forth in the sky, effortlessly like a boat in the water, over the bridge. This orb wanted to be seen.

I was amazed. I didn't know what to make of it. As a child, I'd never heard of UFOs or anything of that sort prior. So I was trying to make sense of what I was seeing, and my description of that was a "mini moon" that floated like a boat on water. Things got more interesting as I observed this object, which the experience in total may have lasted anywhere between fifteen to twenty minutes.

Then things got even more interesting. Two jets were scrambled to pursue this object. They came out of Queens. At this point, I felt like I was in a movie. I couldn't believe what I was seeing. I was excited, and I was scared. I asked my brother to come take a look at it. He was terrified and ran back to his bunk bed and got under the covers. Me, on the other hand, I couldn't take my eyes off it. You might as well have given me popcorn, because my eyes were glued to what I was seeing!

So the jets pursued this object. Then that object just vanished. The jets headed back towards Queens. Then this object reappeared. When it did so, it really started going heavy with the

light show. It started pulsating, and the light was even more brilliant. Things only got more interesting from there.

From the middle of the Whitestone Bridge to my building, I'd say it was somewhere between five to ten miles in distance. So what started happening was that this object, from that point over

the bridge to my neighborhood, started flying over in what appeared to be within seconds. In under a minute, this object flew from the bridge to my neighborhood at least eight times. Back and forth effortlessly, like nothing. It was as fast as if you were to point a laser pointer on a chalkboard and move it around. That's how fast it was.

When it got to my neighborhood, which was very fast, I noticed that it wasn't an orb. It was, in fact, a disc-shaped craft. Metallic in nature. And that orb, which I thought it was just an energy of sorts, was actually around the craft... like an aura of some sort.

That was my first sighting. I couldn't take my eyes off the sky after that, and I became very adamant in observing and watching the skies.

The second sighting took place in late October of 2002. I worked as a security guard for a beer distribution company. This was also in the Bronx. My shift was from 11 p.m. to 8 a.m. I noticed what appeared to be like the sparkles from Roman candles. I started noticing this over this building that was in front of the facility.

I was in my post in the back of the facility. My curiosity got the best of me, and I walked toward the front of the facility to the first post. That facility was as big as a football field. So when I got to the front, I saw, from out the sparks and directly over the building, a triangular craft that appeared out of nowhere. It was big. It was silent. If I didn't see it come out of those sparks, I wouldn't have known it was there in the first place. There was one light on it that was red. Other than that, it completely blended in with the night.

I walked backwards with this triangular craft over me, which by the way, was just over six stories above me. It was fairly close. I was pretty sure that if I wanted to, I could throw something at the object. But I walked backwards the entire time with this object over me, and it was so unreal that I couldn't even talk. I just moved with it backwards until it went over the back of the facility, which was obscured by a big rock wall that went into the Cross Bronx Expressway. And that was it.

Those are my stories. I hope that people in New York share their stories more, because to my understanding, having a sighting out there is not unusual. But we don't hear about those much, especially in the five boroughs.

I hope that changes.

THERE'S SOMETHING IN THE BACKYARD

My name is Daniel Kuster. My UFO sighting was witnessed by myself and my parents. It occurred in a little town approximately sixty-five kilometers, or forty miles, southwest of Sydney, Australia. I have previously reported it to MUFON (Mutual UFO Network), and it was actually investigated by the national director for MUFON Australia in New Zealand, who just by chance happened to have grown up in the same little town that I grew up in just on the outskirts of Sydney, and he actually had a UFO sighting there himself in the 1970s.

My sighting took place on April 6, 1993. Even though it was a long time ago, I did write down the events of the sighting not long after, just so I would have a record of it for myself. It was such an extraordinary event, and I know how memory fades with time, so I wanted to keep a record of what exactly occurred that night. It's basically the same report that I filed with MUFON years later.

So that night, I was sitting in the lounge room of my parents' house, watching TV. My parents were sitting in the back room, also watching TV. And what's bizarre is that one minute, I was wide awake, and the next, I basically just started feeling this overwhelming sense of tiredness and fatigue, like I was about to drop asleep then and there.

So I went up to bed. My bedroom faced out to the backyard, so I had a window that looked out over this yard. My bed was basically directly below the window. I was lying in bed on my side, facing away from the window, and even though I felt this overwhelming sense of tiredness, I was lying there awake for probably ten to fifteen minutes when suddenly, I don't know why, I felt this urge to just turn around and look out the window. So I did.

What I saw was a craft that was completely silent. It was moving from the house over to the backyard. It was a silver metallic color. It basically looked like a typical flying saucer. I couldn't believe what I was seeing. I turned away from the window and then turned back a few times because I thought I was seeing things. Once I established that I was wide awake and that I wasn't seeing things, I went running out to the living room, where my parents were, and told them there was a UFO or something in the backyard.

We went to the kitchen window that overlooked the backyard, and all three of us saw this thing. I wanted to get a closer look, so I decided to go to the backyard. I remember my mom saying something along the lines of, "Don't go out there... you might get abducted!" I basically just laughed and kept going and went out to the backyard. My dad followed me out.

As soon as we walked out to the backyard, maybe five or ten seconds later, this thing started to move off slowly and silently. I got a better look at it and estimated it to be approximately ten to fifteen meters in diameter. Probably from bottom to top, the craft was about two to three meters high and about fifteen to twenty meters above us. So it was very close. It definitely looked like a structured and manufactured craft. A metallic disc-shaped UFO. It had a long, rectangular red light with two square white lights on each side of the red light on the back of the craft. I didn't see any windows or portholes or anything on the craft, and didn't see any dome on top of it. It continued to fly off, gaining in height and speed the farther it got away.

Prior to this sighting, I can't say that I had a great interest in UFOs. I'd obviously heard of them and saw movies about them. So did my mom. You could tell by her comment about getting abducted. I guess, in some way, we're conditioned through media to think that these things are extraterrestrial. But prior to that, I personally had no interest in these things. My dad was a complete skeptic. Doesn't believe in aliens visiting Earth or anything like that.

I can admit that since the sighting, I've developed a keen interest in the topic. I read a lot of books about it, and I have started leaning towards the extraterrestrial hypothesis myself. But not 100%.

To this day, my dad takes the correct position in saying that, even having seen what we did, "I don't know what it was." I don't know what it was either, but it changed my life. In the sense that my interest in not only UFOs, but in the universe as well. Even though I can't say what it was, the more I learn about the topic, it seems the less I know about it! There's such a wealth of information out there, and so many people with different opinions.

I would love to know, before I die, what we saw that night. But for now, all I can say is that I don't know what it was, other than a UFO.

A PHENOMENAL RELATIONSHIP

My name is Monserrat Pineda. I've had what appears to be a lifelong relationship with unidentified flying objects. I was born in Chile in 1961. My father had received a prestigious Rockefeller scholarship, which allowed my family to move to the United States. While he attended university, upon receiving his master's and PhD in veterinary medicine, we returned back home to the Los Rios region of Valdivia, where my family owned a ranch.

On the evening of my first event, my extended family had gathered for a reunion, celebrating our return. After dinner that evening, some of us gathered outside because the power had gone out. The remote landscape was pitch black. Suddenly, a light was noticed through the tree line near the river's edge, traveling and weaving.

While this was happening, our two dogs began barking quite loudly and taking off toward it. I heard an adult in the group wonder aloud, "Who might be coming to visit?" They assumed it was a car, but oddly, that wouldn't make sense, as there was only one road in. And it was nowhere near the river.

Unexpectedly, a bright light appeared overhead. Our group

was mesmerized, looking up. No one said a word. No sound. Just the stillness of the night and a sense of something huge looming overhead. Then, suddenly, this light began to take off, shining below across hundreds of acres. I stood by the barn, along with other children, watching in awe.

My siblings and parents would each later recall being in different parts of the homestead that night. Interestingly, no one could figure out who the other mysterious children were whom I was standing next to.

We heard on the car radio as we headed home that some fishermen a few miles away had encountered an unexplained object the same night. Our family never discussed it until years later after other events unfolded.

Many strange synchronicities would occur over the years. Especially after we came back to the States in the late '60s. Fast-forward to an early morning of January in 2007 after twenty-plus successful years in the corporate world, I now had the privilege of being a stay-at-home mom.

On this particular January morning, like clockwork, I walked my two children down the long driveway in the dark to await the school bus. As they chatted among themselves, looking in the opposite direction, I was mesmerized by a sphere in the sky now weaving and floating towards us. It was softly glowing inside. It was about the size of a basketball, and it was traveling only a few feet above the road towards us.

This sphere began to dematerialize as soon as the school bus rolled in. As my kids boarded the bus, I watched as another sphere traveled over the bus. It then floated over my neighbor's roof, and it disappeared.

After this event, I went inside, and although well rested, and with twenty or more chores to do for the day, I suddenly felt the urge to go lie down for a nap. I awoke four hours later to a sound unlike anything I had ever heard before. The glass windows throughout the house were rattling loudly to the vibration of what sounded like a military helicopter above my roof.

I bolted up, disoriented, and ran downstairs to look. But now there was complete silence. Several hours later, the kids were back from school and were hanging out in the den when suddenly that helicopter sound began again. My windows were rattling again, and by this point, I was pissed off. I was wondering why some idiot in a helicopter was flying so close to my roof. I felt like my windows were going to break, so I ran outside. But again, nothing was there, and the sound had stopped. I was confused and really trying hard to process what was happening.

Later that evening, out to dinner with my husband, I shared these odd events as the kids were playing nearby. On our return home, while everyone else was upstairs getting ready for bed, I was in the kitchen, prepping our lunches for the next day. As I stood by the kitchen window, facing a different pasture that is behind my pool fence, a light of some kind was now traveling slowly along the fence line. It was just a few feet off the ground. It was very luminous, and I watched it in between the fence cracks. I stepped outside quietly, and I went to investigate. Again the sound of a helicopter above. Yet it was pitch dark outside, and there was no sign of any helicopters anywhere.

I did reach out to MUFON on this occasion, and I was informed that three other cases within a few miles of my home had actually been reported on the same day.

I've always felt guided, protected, and even more so now, as on any given day or night, I sense their presence, and I do see their craft often. It is always benevolent for me. It has brought me a deeper and more profound connection to God.

I feel blessed anytime I see them in our skies.

THE ROAD TRIP

My name is Melissa. Back on October 3 of 1995, I had what I can only describe as an unidentified flying object incident. I remember the date precisely because it was the same day that I was moving from Florida to Kansas after my freshman year of college.

That day, it was my mother, my stepfather, and I, in a U-Haul van that I had rented. Interesting side note, the other reason I remember the exact date was because we were listening to the OJ Simpson verdict on the radio.

So we were driving one straight shot, which was about twenty-five hours. We were halfway through, roughly about fourteen hours into the drive, and we were east of St. Louis, Missouri. It was a very dark night, and there wasn't a lot of traffic because it was a weeknight. My stepfather was driving, my mother was in the middle, and I was on the passenger side, looking out the window. I wasn't necessarily paying attention to anything in particular. But then something caught my eye.

There were these lights in the sky. At first, you kind of read-just your eyes a little bit and try to figure out exactly what you're seeing. But I saw distinctly three distinct lights. And the reason they caught my eye was that they weren't moving. But then one would move really slowly, and then another one would move. It was almost like this kind of choreographed movement that was going on between the three. We were far enough away from them where I watched this for a while.

Another thing that struck me was that they were perfectly spaced apart. The lighting on it was kind of sporadic. It was blinking lights, but not like a pulsating light that you normally see on a jet. And they were perfectly spaced apart. But they would sometimes move at the exact same speed, together, or sometimes one would move and the other one would move. And then once in a while, one would just dim completely and be gone. Then I'd look again, and it would be in a different location.

So I was watching this for a while, and I was sitting there, in my head, trying to decide if I should tell my stepfather or not. I remember being really nervous to tell him because he's one of those very skeptical people. He also is someone who has his pilot's license, and he was in the Air Force Reserves. So I thought that he'd probably just dismiss it. But I kept watching it. And then more lights appeared.

I noticed there was one across the interstate on the other side of us. So at that point, it was almost like they were all around. I don't recall how many there were, but the way they were moving... it was almost like there was communication going on between them. They moved very similar to a drone. They would stop for a while, and then one would move. Certainly, back in 1995, there was nothing that existed, to my knowledge at least, that could do that.

I don't remember how long I was watching this all. Maybe several minutes. But I couldn't hold it in any longer. I finally told my stepfather. I asked him, "Do you see those lights?"

I think he noticed them too, and he just didn't want to say anything. He was like, "Yeah. I've been watching them."

I asked him what he thought they were. He said, "I honestly can't tell you. I don't know what that is."

We didn't really say a lot after that, because we were more just in awe and trying to comprehend what we were witnessing. I think my mother was a little more freaked out by it.

We didn't hear any noise, but the vehicle was loud enough to where I wouldn't know if there was any noise associated. They kept staying in view, too. It was almost like they were moving with us. I'm not saying they were following us or anything. I'm just saying it was like they were kind of moving along the same pattern or the same distance along with us. It felt like we watched this for probably twenty minutes or so. As we got closer to St. Louis, I could see the city lights. Or at least the reflection in the sky. And then the lights just disappeared, and that was it.

We're used to very dark nights and skies in Kansas. We've seen a lot of meteor showers and things of that sort. But we just couldn't put a placement to what it was we saw.

Looking back on the whole experience, I honestly don't know what I saw. I have told several people about it. My husband and a couple of family members and some friends of mine who are UFO enthusiasts.

But a couple of years ago, I decided to tell my nephew, who has been an Air Force pilot for over fifteen years. So he's seen a few things, though he won't admit it publicly. When I told him about this incident, he said to me that he had absolutely no doubt that what I saw was real. And that the one thing I should keep in mind is that there are craft that have been created by our military that far exceed our imagination. Maybe what I saw in 1995 is what's available today, like drones. So that was kind of interesting to me. It was also interesting to me that he didn't dismiss or deny what I said. In fact, if anything, he validated it. So that in itself was very reassuring.

THE DAY THE MINI SAUCER CAME

My name is Elle. I'm from Northeast Ohio. I was about seven years old when this sighting occurred in 2001. It was the first I can ever recall, but it certainly wasn't the last.

I loved to play this game in my backyard that I called "Bus Driver." It's exactly what it sounds like: I'd walk around the yard and pretend that I was a bus driver, picking the kids up to go to school. I don't know why it was fun, but I loved doing it. I did it almost every single day.

This particular day, I remember there was something going on inside the house. My mom's family was over, so I went outside and started to play my game. There was a deck on the back of the house that had a set of steps that were right at the back of the house. You could go up the steps and go right inside the door. So when I got close to this deck, something compelled me to look up over my shoulder.

When I did, about thirty feet in the air, not very high off the ground, was the literal definition of a flying saucer. Absolutely the most typical saucer you could possibly imagine. It was incredibly small. Like if there were people inside there, maybe one child could fit. That was how small it was. We lived in a single-level ranch home that my parents had just built, and the craft didn't even clear the chimney.

It's crazy how long the moment went on. Or at least how long it goes on in my memory. There are so many details that I can recall. I remember it was silver, but it wasn't reflective. It had three lights that I could see, and they were turned off. But I could see what colors they would be if they were turned on. One would be blue, one would be yellow, and one would be red.

It was just so small... that's still to this day one of the two things that baffles me most. That and how close it was. I had never experienced anything like this. I had never wanted to. It had never been something that was what I was interested in. I loved Barbies and Hot Wheels. I didn't care about space. I didn't care about aliens. I didn't care about any of that stuff. So for me to see this was odd.

Sometimes in the memories, I can recall a figure or being inside the dome on top of the craft. Sometimes I can't. I'm not sure which it would be. Maybe it was both. Maybe it was something I'm just creating in my mind. But I know what I did see, and I know that it was there in front of me.

Everything was silent. There were no sounds. I don't even know what really compelled me to look up, either, because I was just minding my own business, playing my little bus driver game, and something caused me to look up.

After seeing this tiny flying saucer, I ran inside. I didn't want to be around anything like that. When I got inside, my great-grandmother was standing right there, and she's like, "Oh, you look like you just saw a ghost!"

In response, all I could do was shake my head. I didn't say anything about it to her. At some point, I did tell my parents. My dad didn't believe me. My mom didn't say anything at the time. But I found out later that she most definitely did believe me. My dad thought it was an excuse to not have to go outside, because in the months that followed over that summer, I didn't want to go outside, whether I was with someone or not. I didn't want to see that again. I would sit on the floor of my bedroom with my yellow line tablet and draw this house, this girl, and this flying saucer. Again, it was utterly silent when the incident happened. But when I was drawing these, I would always have some kind of caption on that flying saucer. It would always say something like, "Elle... it's us. We're not here to harm you."

Again, I have to stress that when this happened, I had never known about aliens or abductions or anything like that. So I don't know why I added those little captions on to these pictures. I would hide the pictures. I know, eventually, my mom did see them. But I hid them, and eventually I threw them away because I was embarrassed.

That's how I've felt in the following years since that first sighting. Embarrassed. There have been other sightings. There are many other experiences that should confirm to me that I'm not crazy. But I do feel crazy sometimes.

I used to be so shameless in my teen years. I was so shameless about trying to make people believe in it. I thought that if they heard my story, then they would have to believe it. Because they know me. Why would I lie? Therefore my story, to me, was the most compelling truth to them to make them believe it. I kind of became an outcast, in part because of that belief. Eventually, I kind of just shut up about it. I never really speak about it publicly anymore.

There are other experiences that I've had that shouldn't make me feel so insane. But every single day of my life, I do. I feel crazy for seeing the things that I've seen.

They say, "Seeing is believing." But I guess, sometimes, even seeing it can't make you believe it.

THE BAY AREA RECTANGLE

My name is Elena Cladianos. This event occurred on August 30, 2014, in the San Francisco Bay Area. It was about 4 a.m., and I was in my kitchen, drinking orange juice. I decided to check on my truck in the outdoor lot next door because the gate had been stuck in the open position for a month or so, making every night an opportunity for vandals.

The best vantage point to get a good view is through a west-facing floor-to-ceiling corner window in the living room, where the shade is always drawn about 75%, and the pulley to open it is inconveniently located behind an entertainment center. Being difficult to access, as well as being loud and squeaky when tugged (with a sleeping husband just down the hall), I lay on the floor to take a peek. Tummy side down, legs straight back, elbows on the floor, hands under my chin.

That early morning was so dark, I've often described it as "inky." Nothing illuminated. No streetlights, no windows glowing in the surrounding buildings, no cars on the street. Not even the slightest whiz of traffic coming into San Fransisco from the nearby Bay Bridge. There's just a single, bright light in the window of a nearby dilapidated building. So I grabbed a set of binoculars from my husband's sail bag to investigate.

Not finding any movement inside the lighted window, I turned my gaze back to my truck and then up to the dark sky. Immediately, I saw white lights rapidly twirling downward on a diagonal trajectory in my direction. I thought a jet was falling out of control, but quickly knew with certainty that this wasn't the case. There were no red or green lights. Though I was sure the lights were fixed to an object by their pattern rotation, which slowed as it neared closer. I soon saw that the object was a giant, black rectangle, which had been spinning like a top on its vortex. The spinning stopped, and it glided into a position directly in front of me at my window, straight up and down longways like a big black door, where it hovered above the ground. It had four round white lights, one on each corner, and was completely stable in its hovering state. The lights did not emit a beam, pulsate, or blink. The rectangle did not wobble. I don't recall hearing any sounds at all.

I inspected the rectangle with my binoculars, but there was nothing to see on the surface other than the black "color" and four white lights. The binoculars fogged up, so I put them down, and shortly thereafter it slowly levitated, turned on its side, almost like a "flying carpet," and floated off over the Harrison Street off-ramp. If it continued on that trajectory, it would have flown over the financial district.

I ran to my computer to make a post on Facebook, and I'm so glad I did because it served as a reliable timestamp for the duration of this episode. I know I was drinking OJ in the kitchen at 4 a.m. because I looked at a clock. Rushing to post an update on Facebook, hoping someone would look up and see the rectangle, I know the entire timeline was about fifteen minutes.

At no time did I feel threatened or afraid. I felt peaceful in the dark, quiet morning, and during the incident I was simply awestruck, in a state of wonderment over what was occurring. On my mind were feelings of deep curiosity and gratefulness to be witnessing something so extraordinary and unexplainable.

THE BUBBLING BLACK BLOB OF FIFE

My name is Tommy. I'm from a small town in Fife, Scotland. Its population is around 2,000, and it's a beautiful little corner of the world. My experience happened during the summer of 1996. I was ten years old, and it was around 2 p.m. My friend Jay and I were meeting up with another friend, Ray, who had just arrived home from vacation.

As Jay and I walked along the pathway outside, we noticed something on the ground, glimmering in the sunlight. The closer we got to it, the bigger it seemed to get. Almost as if it were spreading across the road. It looked just like an oil slick. And honestly, that was what we thought it was. It was multicolored and shiny.

Jay had forgotten something at his house, so we went back, thinking nothing of the thing in the road. But when we returned, it had actually grown bigger, stretching from one side of the road all the way to the other. Intrigued, we got closer to get a better look.

We approached it slowly and were instantly hit with the most God-awful smell. I can only describe it as a mixture of burning rubber, nail polish remover, and manure. It made both Jay and me feel nauseous, so we retreated about thirty yards, trying to avoid it.

Suddenly, this giant oil slick, for lack of a better description, started bubbling and smoking. Within a few seconds, it began to rise from the ground. We were terrified. It made the most terrible sound I had ever heard. Thinking about that still gives me chills. It sounded like metal chains in a washing machine, being accompanied by a choir of screaming animals. Only louder and more violent. It physically hurt our ears.

I remember standing there with both hands covering my ears while witnessing what happened next. It suddenly shot up from the road. Within seconds, it must have been about forty-five to fifty feet in the air. It still looked like a multicolored oil slick, but had gotten even bigger. It also now took on an almost transparent quality.

Everything behind it, or through it, took on a strange mix of color. Against the blue summer sky, it was extremely jarring. The thing was still bubbling and smoking. We stood there frozen in terror, unable to take our eyes off it. It hovered in the sky above us for what felt like forever, when suddenly, it rose higher into the sky, then shot off in the distance, making a terrifying, world-ending noise. It left a purplish-black trail in the sky behind it, which seemed to take ages to disappear. The odor was still noticeable, albeit much fainter than before.

The thing stopped in the sky above the river, next to a hillside farm on the edge of town. At this point, it looked more like a giant, black smudge in the sky, and it appeared to be surrounded in smoke or some sort of dark haze. It hovered in place for a few seconds. Then out of nowhere, a massive bright yellowish-green beam of light shone down from the sky above it and surrounded it in the brightest light I had ever seen. What sounded like a huge metallic thunderclap reverberated from the distance. The massive beam of light lit up even brighter; then it disappeared as quickly as it had been there. The smoking black thing was gone without a trace.

Jay and I stood in the middle of the road, frozen in absolute shock and terror. So much so that we were almost run down by an oncoming ice-cream truck. By this point, the weather had turned. It was overcast, and it had started to rain. We decided we didn't want to go to Ray's house anymore, because honestly, we were both so shaken. We turned around and began to walk back to my house when the town clock chimed four times. This meant it was 4 p.m. We assumed the clock must be broken because it had only chimed 2 p.m. a few moments earlier.

We arrived to my home, and my mum told us that Ray had called several times looking for us. Confused, I called him back. He was pretty upset and asked why we hadn't gone to his house. He was pretty angry. I was utterly baffled, and I had no idea what he was talking about. We had literally just been on our way to see him. I looked at the clock in my parents' living room, and it read 4:05 p.m. I asked my mum what the correct time was, and you guessed it. She said it was 4:05 p.m.

Not only had Jay and I witnessed something completely strange and unnatural, but we had somehow also lost two hours of time.

THE RURAL RHOMBUS OF MAINE

My name is Jakob Cullins. This story takes place in the autumn of 2015 in a rural part of central Maine. It happened on my family's property on the top of a hill. The population of our town is about 4,000. Pretty small. The property is about a square acre, and the house is right about in the center of that acre. The yard around it is fairly sizable. On three sides, it's surrounded by woods.

I was home alone, and I took my dogs out to the backyard at around 11 p.m. so that they could go to the bathroom and so that I could smoke a cigarette. This was a nightly thing at the time, and nothing weird had ever happened. Until this night.

We were outside for maybe five minutes. The dogs finished doing their business, and I finished my cigarette. I walked them right up to the back porch. And as soon as the dogs crossed the threshold into the house from the back porch, I heard this really weird humming noise coming from just above me in the sky. It almost sounded engine-like. I guess I could compare it to the sound of a boiler room when the heat kicks on. Like a strange reverberating, low-frequency hum. It immediately got my attention, as it seemed to fill my ears, drowning out all other noise.

The dogs didn't seem to notice the sound. I mean, I wasn't exactly focused on their reaction at all, but it did seem like they didn't pay it any mind. So I let them inside and turned around to see what was making the noise.

When I looked up, I saw this rhombus-shaped, 3-D diamond. The nose end of it was longer than the tail end. And it was just hovering above the tree line. Maybe just a couple of feet above the trees. So really only about thirty feet or so above the ground. The whole texture of the thing was just this seamless black glass. And the edges of the rhombus were all kinds of lit up. Almost like an LED strip. That's the closest thing I could describe it like. It was edged out with all these little sparkling lights.

This object was slowly making its way across my yard. I just remember being completely frozen, both with fear and in awe-like wonderment. It was just sort of sauntering very slowly. It looked very large and dense, and it didn't seem like something that could hover like that. Just this giant thing. So it just glided right along the trees.

The other thing that I noticed was that the trees didn't move at all. I would imagine if it was a giant drone or something, then there would have been kind of like a vortex created by the propellers that kept it up. It would have moved the trees around. But there was nothing. It was not interacting with the world around it at all. It was like it was there, but doing its own thing. I found this very strange.

It was coming from the right side of the tree line. Over the course of a couple of seconds, it floated away from me at the same speed, to the point where I couldn't see it behind the trees. After a certain point, and I remember it maybe lasted about twenty seconds of this thing making its presence known, I remember making a very strong conscious effort not to blink, look away, or even flinch. In the moment, I knew how important this experience was, and I needed to do everything in my power to face up to it. That's about as rational as I can make it.

I was completely frozen in fear. I didn't know what was going to happen. I could imagine being a bear in the woods. And all of a sudden this giant, metal bird flies down, and people come out of it, and they shoot you with this weird dart gun. Then you pass out and wake up, and you've been tagged. And you have no idea what just happened. I wasn't sure if I was about the be abducted or something. So that's kind of how I felt. Like a grizzly bear possibly about to be tagged by researchers or something!

So the object slowly got farther away from me. I could still hear it, but I couldn't see it anymore. The farther away it got, the lighter the sound got. And then after that, I just went inside.

What's so strange to me sometimes is that you still have a whole life to live after something like that. This insane thing just happened to you, but you still have to go to school or work. Pay the bills. Cook dinner. I remember just going inside that night and just watching TV and playing video games. Like this thing just didn't happen to me. I think it took a little while for it to really set in.

A lot of memories are fuzzy for me, but that is forever burned into my brain. The exact way it happened. It was how it looked. How it sounded and how it moved. I don't really tell very many people in my life. Told some friends and family before, but that's about it. Luckily, nobody thinks I'm crazy.

Nothing like that ever happened since. I still live at the same location, and I haven't seen anything. I definitely keep my eye out for it, but it hasn't returned. It's just this really weird thing that happened that lasted no more than twenty seconds. This thing came out of nowhere and said, "Hello..." and then just took off. And I have no explanation.

I've been racking my brain ever since.

CATCH OF THE DAY

My name is Terry Nattress. I live in Northumberland in Northern England. The following incident took place on June 25, 1978, when I was twenty-eight years old.

I had started packing my gear to go fishing and was running a bit late to catch the turn of the tide at noon that day. The weather was fine. Not a cloud in sight. I've been a photographer for many years and nearly always carried a camera with me on the weekends. So I placed my camera in my bag as usual, but had second thoughts and put it back in the cupboard. It was probably one of the biggest mistakes I have ever made.

I was traveling north on the A189 from Cramlington to Lynemouth Power Station, close to where I was going to fish. That was where I spotted an unusual object just above the horizon to the left of the road. It was sort of a zeppelin shape. My first thought was that it was an air balloon of some sort. That was until I caught a better view of it about a mile farther down the road.

I pulled up into a lay-by, got out of my car, and studied the object for about a minute. And I realized it was moving very slowly to the west, about ten degrees above the horizon. I then considered that maybe this was not a balloon after all. It had a strange-colored swirl of light that it was emitting. The only way I can really describe it is sort of a liquid gas, which seemed to be covering this perfect symmetrical shape, like a cigar.

I got back in the car and drove farther up the road about three miles until the object came into view again. Then I got out of the car and stood to watch it. That was when I noticed that it had begun to diminish in size. I then realized it was actually turning around. I watched as it performed a complete 180-degree turn, which took about forty-five seconds. Then it started moving east towards the sea.

It was difficult to make out an exact shape, but it seemed to resemble the rear of a submarine.

As it was turning, the swirling colored substance was covering the object like a screen over the entire surface, but never interfering with its perfect shape. I ruled out the possibility of it being a gas cloud, as the movements were in a controlled manner. I also came to the definite conclusion that it was not a balloon and was unlike anything I'd ever seen before.

I decided to race up the motorway towards the power station about five miles away. I pulled up next to the gates where I usually park the car. The object was in and out of view on the way, but by the time I arrived to the power station, it had turned around again and was now heading west. I was now much closer to the object than before. And it was huge!

It was moving behind the pylon, so I had a scale of distance I could use to determine how far away it was. It must have been less than half a mile from me. I stood and watched the object for over five minutes until it slowly went out of view.

The swirling substance effect was something I still find difficult to describe. But the nearest description I would say would be a very intense, condensed light of blue, orange, and yellow mixed together in a swirly massive energy that seemed to cover the entire cigar shape. There was no sound the entire duration of the sighting.

The sighting from start to finish was about fifteen to twenty minutes. Frustratingly, there was no one else around, and I had left my camera at home.

I couldn't do anything more that day in terms of the sighting, so I elected to do what I originally set out to do: go fishing!

I decided to go down to the beach about a hundred yards away from where I parked the car, and there was one solitary fisherman down there. I set the rod up and cast off, asking this other fisherman to watch my rod. I then went up to some nearby sand dunes to see if the object had possibly come back. I didn't see anything. So I returned to my rod and asked the fisherman if he'd seen anything in the sky. He shook his head no but then asked me if I'd seen a UFO! Apparently there had been a string of sightings in the area as of late.

After chatting some more, we saw about a dozen light aircraft circle the area. I would say quite dangerously because they were very close to one another. The other fisherman and I found this quite strange, as if they had been alerted to something in the area. Could it have been because of what I'd seen?

I left that day with no fish. However, I did leave with a lasting memory of that cigar-shaped craft in the sky.

A NEW YEAR IN CAPE TOWN

My name is Simon Tatt. I live in Cape Town, South Africa. My interest in UFOs started in the mid-1980s. I was born in the UK, and I went back to visit family. And that was when one of my aunts gave me a book on the Betty and Barney Hill UFO incident. I'd never heard of it before. It was an absolutely fascinating book to read, and it got me interested in UFOs. I keep an open mind and find it a great subject.

So my sighting took place in Cape Town on January 1 of 2017, at about twelve past midnight. I was actually house-sitting for a friend. They had a couple of dogs, and there was just a bit of worry when they went out to their New Year celebrations that the dogs might be disturbed by the fireworks going off. So I agreed to house-sit and take care of the dogs.

The house is up on a hill on the slopes of Table Mountain, a national park here in Cape Town.

I had just finished watching the fireworks display, which had just died down. And I just happened to glance up and notice a sort of circular wireframe shape in the sky. It was two-dimensional, and the color was a pinkish orange. It was moving fairly quickly from southwest to northeast in a rough direction, over a saddle between Table Mountain and Lion's Head, two points of interest in Cape Town.

Immediately following the circular shape was a triangle. Also pinkish orange in color. And right behind that was a long, oblong shape. Same colors. All of the shapes were rotating slowly, or they were wobbling slightly on a common axis. They all appeared to be hollow. No solid form to them at all. Just outlines. They appeared to all be in a straight line, and they were undulating or wobbling slightly from side to side. But all of them moved along this common axis in line, one behind the other.

The last sight that I had was of the oblong object disappearing from view behind some trees. The oblong object was moving on a flat plane, but moving very much like those military ship's radar devices, which slowly move around.

Altitude-wise, I'd say probably between seven hundred to one thousand feet above where I was sitting. Difficult to really judge exactly how high they were and what size. But if I had to guess the size, maybe about twenty-five feet across each object. There was absolutely no noise from any of the objects at all.

I did look in the newspapers and online the next day to see if anything similar had been reported. I didn't see anything. I don't know what they were, but I'm quite familiar with aircraft. So I'm pretty sure they weren't helicopters or drones. It would be odd to have drones over that area, three of them, one behind the other in those shapes as well. I could imagine drones over the harbor while the fireworks were going off at midnight, but this was at least twelve minutes after midnight.

I've never seen anything that's proven either way that these were or were not man-made objects. I don't know whether they were from another dimension or planet, or whether they were something man-made that I just don't know about.

The next day, I wrote up a report for a South African UFO website. Funnily enough, I noticed there was another UFO sighting at twelve past midnight. Though, that sighting occurred in Johannesburg, almost nine hundred miles away. Its description was not the same as mine, either. It just so happened to be at the same exact time as I reported. I suppose being New Year's Eve that there would be a lot of lights in the sky. And I suppose if any alien entity wanted to sort of disguise their actions in the New Year, this would be a good time to bring out a brightly lit craft.

Whatever those objects were, I'd never seen anything like them before or since. But no matter what they were, I just feel very lucky to have seen them.

CONFIRMATION IN NORWAY

My name is Benedikt Örn Hjaltason. I'm originally from Iceland, but I've been living in Norway for the past thirty years. I'm currently a technology student. I had a pretty crazy experience in 2010. At that point, I was already very into UFOs. I was researching, and I was actually writing a blog about it. I was also into paranormal and occult magick ritual stuff. Something called sigil magick. This is a kind of technique that you use to try to manifest something in your life. And I wanted to use this ritual to try to make contact with UFOs or extraterrestrials.

Sometime after this, I was getting ready to go to work at a hotel where I worked night shifts. It was late this night, and the minute I pulled up my curtains, I could see this glowing object in the sky. I knew straight away that it was something extraordinary. I looked at it for a few seconds, and then I ran out to the driveway.

When I got to the driveway, I saw there were three of these objects in the same area of the sky. They were just glowing orbs of light. Kind of golden, reddish. Very intense glowing lights. They were moving slowly around the same area, and they were playing with each other. They made a right-angle triangle on five different occasions. They would almost power up to this insane intensity. Also, they would hold this new intensity for maybe six to nine seconds, and then they would go down again. The power-up sequences made me feel like there was this enormous amount of energy being channeled into our reality. Like there was some kind of reservoir being pumped in it. It was like all the colors of the spectrum, just radiating at once.

From that point, they were kind of putting on a show for me. One of the things that I remember the best is that they were kind of fading in and out. Sometimes it was a fade-out, and then it would come back into reality. So this maneuver that I remember is that one of them would fade in at one place, and another one would fade in a little bit above and to the right. It would then move over the first one. And the moment it was just above the first one, the lower one would light up to that insane intensity. Looking at these was like looking at a hot coal.

I would say that I watched these objects for almost ninety minutes in total. I was standing outside in the cold, just watching this. And when they were lighting up, I just kind of screamed with joy. It was just so intense for me. But this wasn't the end of the experience. It would end with three military planes.

These planes were propeller-driven. They came from the direction behind me. They were flying very low. The middle one flew maybe about five hundred meters straight above my head.

And they were going in the direction of these objects. The middle plane, which flew over my head, flew in a straight line on a collision course towards one of the stationary objects. It flew extremely close to it. I was standing on the ground there, and I was afraid that it was going to crash into it. But at the last second, the airplane very abruptly turned to the right. I think it must have turned as fast as this type of airplane could turn. It looked very dramatic, and you can just imagine three of these big planes flying low over the town. It was like a scene out of a movie.

Shortly after these planes came and confronted them, I reluctantly had to go to work, so I had to leave the area.

There were a lot of things that point me in the direction that this experience was put on for me. Personally, I know it sounds crazy, but it's the only thing that makes sense to me. I did this magick ritual to try to attract this experience, and then it happened. I think it was kind of a demonstration and that this wasn't a random event. Another thing that makes me think this is that the window I first looked out to see them the first time, there are a lot of trees in front of that window. So there's actually a very little patch of clear sky, and this UFO was in the middle of this patch. Also, sometime while I was standing there watching this, I had a good view, in general, but I felt that if I walked a little bit down the street, I would have an even better view. So I tried to walk down the street, but then they just disappeared. So the moment I walked back to my driveway, it started up again with the show. The last thing is that the maneuvers they did... it really looked like they were performing something like on a screen for me.

I've tried many times over the years to get some answers from the military here in Norway, but they're not sharing anything. They're not even lying to me and telling me that it was some kind of exercise. There's just no trace of this, uh, this incident. I'm convinced those planes were military planes. They were three gigantic propeller-driven planes. And doing these kinds of maneuvers... I just don't think a civilian plane or planes would do something like that. Actually, it makes me feel that they did something very risky by flying into this unknown object in the sky. They had no idea what this object was going to do. So doing this over a populated area feels very risky to me.

I'm glad I got to see something as extraordinary as this. In the end, for me, I was convinced of the reality of UFOs. This event was a huge confirmation for me. A confirmation that this phenomenon is real.

LAKE ERIE

M y name is Mark Brabant. This event happened in 1991. I can't believe it's been nearly thirty years, but it has. And I still think about it quite a bit.

So at the time, my buddy Todd and I were in our early twenties. Todd had become part owner of a small boat that was docked in Lorraine, Ohio, which is about thirty miles west of Cleveland, on Lake Erie.

One evening that summer, the two of us took the boat out of the marina, and we were just cruising around, listening to music, and stopping to fish on occasion. Basically, just enjoying a summer night on the water. It was super calm that night. There were no waves. And if there was any wind, it was minimal. It was probably about 10 p.m. It was dark. We were sitting about half a mile offshore. With the motor cut, we were in the back of the boat, chilling, facing east. That was when we saw something in the sky.

There was this small white light maybe fifty yards to the southeast. I'm estimating, but that seems to be pretty accurate. The light looked to be just off the surface of the water. It was kind of hard to tell at first sighting. It didn't look very big, but it was blinking on and off, rhythmically and consistently. Maybe in one-and-a-half-second increments. As we watched, it looked like it was coming towards us. We could tell it wasn't very big at all. And it was making no noise. We were both commenting like, "What the hell is this thing?" The usual things you would say when you're looking at something that you don't understand.

The light was a pure white, and it was spherical. When it wasn't on, in between blinks, you couldn't see any outline or shape, so it was very hard to tell what this thing actually looked like, if it had a shape at all.

It continued towards us on a perfectly straight line, and it wasn't changing altitude. It wasn't changing its height whatsoever. And it was probably three feet above the water. So as it got closer, we were watching it intently. We were standing up, trying to make sense of this thing coming at us. And it got probably within ten feet of the stern of the boat as it passed by. You could tell that it was maybe the size of a tennis ball. We kept listening for sound, and there was none. We also were watching for any deviation in its flight path that it was on. But it never deviated at all.

We just continued to watch it, wide-eyed, as it flew northwest on the same line until it was out of sight over the horizon in the dark.

To this day, I have no clue what this thing was.

Todd and I are still friends. We still keep in touch regularly, and we revisit the event on occasion. And when we do, neither of us have any more clarity now than we did back then. We just shake our heads over it.

I've always been interested in the UFO topic and have kept up with a lot of sighting reports. And I've yet to come across a similar sighting. I wonder what this thing was, and I still think about it today.

IN THE CLOUDS

My name is Stella Gardiner. My dad got me into UFOs when I was a child. He actually bought UFO books and brought them home. We also watched documentaries together and even drove out to UFO hot spots at times to see if we could see something. We never did.

Until this event.

This is my first ever UFO experience that occurred in Plymouth, England. This was in the late '70s when I was nine or ten. It had to be in summer because it was still quite light out, and it was later in the evening. I was allowed to stay out a bit later in the summer, and I remember the sky being really blue that night.

I was in the park with my sister next to Laira Railway Depot. I happened to look up in the sky. That was when I saw a glassy ball-shaped orb of some sort. It was a large distance away at first and then got close. That was when I noticed it was disc-shaped and giving off light. It moved from green to blue to red. That went on for quite a long time as well.

At some point, I noticed I wasn't the only person watching. There was maybe around a dozen kids and parents watching this object as well. I remember one kid asked his dad what it was, and the dad said, "Oh, it's nothing." But I knew it clearly was something. And because of my interest in UFOs, I was determined to stay watching it, to see how it ended. I think my sister probably wasn't that interested and wanted to go home, but I didn't want to go.

I'm not sure the time involved, but it felt like a very long time that we were standing there, watching it. At some point, there was a cloud being blown along towards the object. So there was otherwise blue sky and this one cloud. It was moving in a very straight line towards the object until it actually covered it. I could no longer see the disc or the lights. Just the cloud. And it stopped. The cloud literally just stopped and stayed in one place.

After a few more moments, a plane flew out of the cloud. But I hadn't seen any plane fly in. If a plane had gone in, I would have seen it!

This plane just carried on, going across the sky. I can't remember what happened to the cloud, whether it dissipated or whether it was still there. But the plane moved north towards Dartmoor and vanished. Not into the distance... but just disappeared out of existence.

After this event, I went home and told my parents. My dad said he was envious, as he had yet to ever see a UFO. In fact, he said he was a bit annoyed that he wasn't there, and that I'd seen one without him.

I drew the whole thing out using my colored pens, and I wrote a description of it. I never reported it. I think, in the end, I just wasn't sure whom I could report it to or who'd be interested. And I just let it go. I told quite a few people at the time whom I thought I could trust. I remember trying to tell people at school and get my sister to corroborate it all. But she said she didn't remember it happening. I think she just didn't want to talk about it.

Months after, I ended up reading *The Mothman Prophecies* by

John Keel, and there was a case in there of a UFO simply getting covered up by a cloud and then a biplane flying out of it. And I remember thinking that it sounded just like my sighting! And I got a little excited by that because it wasn't that long after the book had come out that I had my sighting.

I've seen other things since, but this was the first and by far the best thing I had seen.

FINDING LIGHT THROUGH THE DARK

My name is Dalia Monterroso. This event happened in 1997. I was a social worker, working in a camp that was for kids. It was basically like a detention center out in the middle of the desert in Elfrida, Arizona, which is very close to the border of Mexico. Really just the middle of nowhere.

So both the kids and the staff lived at the camp. The way it was set up was that there was an area where the kids stayed, and then there were the dormitories where the staff lived. And there was a little path that went from the staff housing to the area where the kids lived. And the path was not lit. It was pretty dark.

So I was walking with another staff member along this path one night. It was so dark and clear out. Not a single cloud in the sky. You could see every single star. So this staff member and I were talking as we went down the path, and then, for whatever reason, we both stopped and looked up. And I don't know why we did that, but we did. And something caught our attention.

There were three lights in the sky, and they were very far away. At first, we thought maybe it was a plane. But then the three lights moved away from each other. So that was very strange. And I was thinking, *Wait a minute… what is that?* The lights moved away from each other. So unless it was, like, an aircraft that was stretching or something... but I don't know of any aircraft that does that. It just didn't make any sense.

We knew at that point that we were looking at three separate objects. We were just kind of standing there, and we were not really saying anything. And then, all of a sudden, the lights went back into a triangular formation, and they just took off across the sky!

We just stood there. I remember feeling very confused. We just started making our way towards the camp where the kids were, which was where we were going in the first place. And as we came up to the clearing, a few of the kids came running up. And these were teenagers from the inner city. Kids who were there because they had committed serious crimes. And one of the kids came up, and he was like, "Miss D, did you see that UFO!?"

I told him I had seen it. The other kids also started asking about it as well, and we all started talking about it. There was a feeling of excitement in the camp. But it was also subdued. No matter what we saw, we were still in the situation where these kids were incarcerated, and we were working with them. It was a very difficult situation, so there was this feeling of, *Well... we just saw a UFO in the sky, but it doesn't really change our situation. We are in charge of these kids.*

I have to be honest. I have wanted my whole life to see a UFO. And I've always been curious about them. But in this moment, when we had actually seen one, I don't know how to describe how I felt about it. Because it was almost like, "Okay, yeah... there was a UFO in the sky. Of course there was." It wasn't anything like this big amazement where we were all just freaking out all night over it or anything. It was almost like it was always supposed to be there, and we were supposed to see it. And now, we just had to get back to this difficult situation and life that we were living at that time.

I will say this: That camp was an absolutely horrible place.

There was a lot of abuse there. There was racism there, and it was a terrible situation. I don't believe any of that is going on there anymore, which is a good thing, obviously. But it was such a bad situation that there was always this feeling that the people who were running the place were constantly trying to dehumanize the kids. And my job was to advocate for the kids, which was a very difficult job.

This all just really makes me feel their humanity even more than I did before. Even though we were in this little universe together, where things were really awful and the roles were unjust, we were still just little tiny humans on Earth, looking up in the sky and seeing something that we didn't understand. In that moment, we were complete equals, and we had experienced something truly extraordinary.

THE BROTHERS BROCK

My name is Jesse Brock. I witnessed something that I cannot explain when I was in high school with my younger brother. It was 2008. When I was in tenth grade and my brother was in sixth grade, we lived in an area that is not super rural Tennessee, but it's definitely off the beaten path. We were surrounded by a lot of trees on my parents' ten-acre plot of land. The closest house was maybe two hundred yards away. Pretty remote, too. Rarely heard any cars.

So one night, my brother came and knocked on my door. It was probably shortly after midnight. And I remember my brother would do this thing where he would just knock and wouldn't say who was there. And it would always freak me out. So I was like, "Hello?" and then he said, "Hey, it's me." So I walked out, and he proceeded to tell me that there was something outside. When I asked him what he meant by "something," he told me, "In the sky. It's a triangle."

So we went to his bedroom window and looked out. There was a stretch of about twenty yards or so before a tree line. Then it was just solid woods for acres and acres.

I didn't see the triangle anywhere. He then told me that it was there, and it was hovering over that area of yard up above the tree line with three orange lights on each of the corners and then one large orange light that was glowing in the middle. He also said it was huge and completely silent. Again, I was looking everywhere in the sky, and I didn't see anything. But he assured me that it would come back. And sure enough, it did.

Out of nowhere, this large orange light appeared above the tree line. Then it came very slowly towards our yard and in front of us, directly out the window. It then went over to the left and then disappeared over the tree line. It was completely silent. I could tell it was a large shape, but I couldn't see the three corners that my brother had first described. But whatever it was, it just vanished. And that was the extent of it.

I would describe myself as an avid UFO believer. I was very interested in aliens and the prospect of life from somewhere else in the universe. Or even from another place on our planet. When I had that experience with my brother, I was blown away. It really solidified my belief, and I've never wavered from it since.

My brother and I don't share the same beliefs. He's very skeptical. But the important thing about our sighting is that we've always told the same story. I definitely knew that what we saw was strange, but as we've seen technological progress over the years, the event just seemed stranger and stranger to me.

I believe that whatever the phenomenon is, it's much larger than we could possibly understand. Without having insider information, as it seems there are organizations that have insider information, I think that we're experiencing something real. Especially with the events that have taken place over the past few years with the Navy UFO sightings and the Pentagon's involvement with the UFO issue. It's nice to have this affirmation coming from the US government and highly qualified pilots talking about these sightings. It's comforting and makes me feel a lot better about what I saw.

A SCIENTIST'S RECKONING

My name is Reggie from San Antonio, Texas. I am a science teacher with a background in biology and physics. That being said, I never thought deeply into UFO stories, as they were always considered "woo" in my opinion.

However, in these past few years, I kind of changed my whole perspective after experiencing some weird sightings. And even hearing some weird sightings. Especially from my parents. So I thought I'd share some that changed my whole perspective.

My first sighting was in November of 2020 when I was on my way to work one day. There was something that caught my attention maybe a few miles away and a couple of hundred feet in the air. This object was metallic. The sun was shining on it and gave a little glare. I could make out the shape as spherical, but it looked like it was spinning a little bit. I thought at first it could maybe be a balloon. But then it started moving and really made me question what it was. It then started moving left and right. And then it went up vertically, and it just seemed to disappear, as if somebody just snapped their fingers and made it vanish into thin air. It was just very perplexing.

My other sighting occurred in early 2022. I was sitting outside one evening, and something caught my attention in the sky. It was a bright light. So I thought maybe satellites, a meteor, a plane... something like that. But since the light was really bright, I could not pinpoint what exactly it was. It didn't move like a satellite. It didn't look like space debris. I don't know if it was three objects, but I saw three lights blinking or pulsating, but very slowly. These three lights were in three different locations, too, so I didn't know if the object was one object or three different objects.

Again, being someone who has a science background, I've always dismissed these things as mistaken objects. And many are. And while I still think maybe at least the lights to what I saw could be something we have made, my first sighting... the way it defied physics, it makes me really question what I saw.

Hearing the stories of others also made me really have an open mind because I know they believed what they saw. And it could be very much real. Such was the case when I heard an interesting story from my parents.

When my dad was in the US Navy in the '70s, he saw different types of lights while he was on a ship. He'd be out in the middle of the ocean. It would be during the day and night. He would see these big bright orbs. They had different hues such as blue or orange. But the way they moved was strange.

There was one particular story he had of these orbs during the middle of the day. He saw this bright light move really quickly, and it just stopped and then dropped vertically down into the ocean!

He tried to report it and, of course, was easily shot down. His superiors told him that he didn't see anything and that if he did report it higher up, that he'd possibly be court-martialed or even worse, kicked out of the military with no benefits. Basically suggesting that his entire military career would be over.

So for those reasons, he never mentioned it until recently. He wanted to share it because the stigma of reporting these things has changed so drastically in the past few years. So this story from my dad was just one of those strange stories.

My mother also had a very interesting story she shared with me. This happened within the last several years. It was similar to my first sighting, in the sense that what she saw looked like a metallic flying saucer. My mother was on her way to work early one morning. She was in her car at a four-way stop when she saw something rising above the tree line. It was saucer-shaped, and it was spinning. It seemed to rise vertically and then quickly shot up in the air and just disappeared.

As for my personal sightings, they did change my whole perspective on these phenomena that people report. I'm not 100% convinced that these are "alien," however. There could be something else that we just don't know. And considering we're barely scratching the surface of modern physics, including quantum physics and string theory, it's just really hard to say.

Until we get more understanding of the universe, bigger and smaller, I guess it's just hard to say. But I'd like to share what one notable scientific figure, theoretical physicist Avi Loeb, has been saying recently. He's made some interesting points that we're kind of in the same era that Galileo was where he shared his accounts of what he thought to be true based on what he saw in his telescopes. But his colleagues dismissed his ideas because they had their own understanding. Their own bias. And they weren't open to getting the data. They just dismissed it and called Galileo crazy. But it's clear he wasn't. So to just dismiss these things is silly and absurd.

So the more we understand, the better we can wrap our heads around what's going on in the world and the universe. Regardless of what these sightings may be, they alter one's worldview and even the universe. But probably the best option is to keep a modest approach and gather data so we can know what these things are.

Possibly.

DAS DREIECK ÜBER HUDE

My name is Patrick Bruns. I live in Germany. In 2008, I had a close encounter with a triangular UFO with my friend. This happened during our summer vacation. We spent a lot of time together in a village named Hude, in Northern Germany. We often stayed up very late, and one night we decided to go for a walk. It was already after midnight, and at this time, there were hardly any people out in the area. We walked on a deserted two-lane country road on the bike path, surrounded by fields.

Suddenly, I noticed an object moving directly in our direction, from the right, above the field. I pointed this out to my friend, and we both stood spellbound. This object floated right over our heads, across the road, and very slowly without making any sound. It was dark, maybe black, and was in the shape of an equilateral triangle. It was clearly a solid object. We only saw its underside, sadly. In each of the corners was a round, whitish light. There was also a round light in the center. But it was kind of different. I can't remember the exact color of it. It didn't shine brightly. None of the lights did, actually. They were dim, as if not wanting to be noticed or tying to blend in. It seemed to me that the UFO was flying so low that I could have thrown a rock at it.

When we saw the triangle, I said straight to my friend that it must be a UFO, since I had seen similar objects before in *The X-Files* series. I seemed to react a lot more to the sighting than my friend did. Strangely, although I had a camera phone in my pocket, I didn't think to take it out to capture this. On the one hand, I had the thought that the object might notice this, and I might get into trouble. Who knows? And on the other hand, I didn't want to miss a second with my own eyes.

On the other side of the road, there was a very tall row of trees that would eventually obscure the triangle. So we didn't follow it any farther and couldn't observe it from there anymore. After it left our sight, we both got very scared and quickly ran back to my friend's house in a panic. It was very scary.

I've had several other unexplainable experiences in my life. And I saw this close encounter as a sign that my previous experiences weren't imaginary. However, the triangular UFO topped everything. Especially because I hadn't seen it alone.

Years later, in late 2017, I reported this to a local German UFO reporting office. They visited me at home in Berlin at the time and interviewed me twice for several hours; however, it was never determined what it was we saw.

I no longer have any contact with my friend. However, when I met with him in 2018, he confirmed to me that we had indeed seen this UFO. But he doesn't seem to want to talk much about it himself. I don't know if he's not interested or if it scares him. I no longer have any contact with him today, unfortunately.

If a government really possesses such technology and keeps it secret just to protect its own interests, it would be a crime against humanity, in my opinion, because it could change the entire world for the better! If it really is a national security issue for the country to keep alien-like technology secret in order to be able to defend itself, if the worst comes to worst, then the public will never be officially aware of their existence. It will always remain secret under the pretense of national security.

I'm neither a scientist nor a specialist, but seeing this object stimulated my imagination. Whether it was classified human military technology or nonhuman technology, just knowing that something like this can exist is such a big thing to me. Aliens... time travelers... beings from another dimension... or even holograms or at least an unexpected secret breakthrough in earthly technology. Who knows what these things are?

I think everything is possible.

A COSMIC BORDER CROSSING

My name is Patrick Neitzel. I'm from Dresden in Germany, and I am a customs police officer. This story takes place on July 25, 2013, in Southwest Germany. It happened literally on the border of France.

At approximately 10:30 p.m. that night, my ex and I went outside to have a cigarette. We had a house with a pool, so we were sitting by the pool, just talking like always. And suddenly, I noticed three oddly bright stars in the corner of my eye, hovering above where France would have been.

I looked over my shoulder, and in that moment when I looked up at the stars, these three lights quickly descended in a straight line and then BOOM! There, above me, was a solid, pitch-black triangular craft hovering completely silent. It had to be only about thirty feet above our heads.

It appeared as though this craft was almost looking down at us, belly first, as the lights were pointed towards us. Each side of the triangle was approximately thirty feet. The lights in each corner were extremely bright, but not blinding.

We were absolutely gobsmacked. Like deer caught in the headlights, or if you would encounter a bear in the wilderness.

You turn around, and there's a bear... so you just freeze. We felt absolutely paralyzed, as if we were hypnotized or controlled. I'm not saying that we were, but that's just how it felt. Frozen and staring in disbelief.

Everything had fallen deathly silent during this. Before the triangle appeared, we could hear frogs and crickets all around us. But then complete silence. It was just this triangle, existing in that moment, as if time had stopped. Oddly enough, neither one of us could remember how long the event lasted. It could have been five seconds... three minutes... half an hour. We just don't remember.

We watched as the triangle began to move very quickly from left to right, zigzagging like a Ping-Pong ball. Suddenly, it just shot off towards space in an instant! It moved so fast that it left a trail of light behind it. During all of this, it made no sound whatsoever.

We immediately turned our heads towards each other. We had to confirm that we had really just seen what we'd seen. And what we'd seen was a black triangle. We looked up again, looked at each other, and didn't have to say a word. We both instinctively ran inside the house. In that moment, reality had kicked in. Fight or flight, as it were. I remember being very scared in that instant because I did not know what happened. However, my curiosity quickly took over again, and I went back outside.

I looked up, searching the skies for the triangle. But it never returned.

I didn't choose to have this sighting. But yeah, it happened. It was a blessing because I feel lucky to have seen it. But, as they say, maybe the blessing is also a curse. Because many people just don't believe you. Some choose ridicule, which was very hard, because I know what happened, and they just laugh it off. But with time, I mostly got over that.

I used to be pretty atheistic. I made fun of religion in my younger years. So in that sense, I definitely deserve the ridicule I got from other people. It didn't make me religious, but I am very open-minded now.

Since the 2017 *New York Times* article on UFOs that went viral, that's when my interest in UFOs really kicked in. It's now a daily part of my life. Since going public about this UFO sighting, I lost some friends. But I've also found new ones. I've connected with people who have had similar experiences, so I'm very grateful for that.

I will not claim that what we saw that night was extraterrestrial because I simply have no way of knowing or confirming that. All I know is that I know nothing.

I hope that one day, we will have something like disclosure where everybody will accept the reality of this, whatever it may be.

The phenomenon is real. And that night changed my life forever.

A PHENOMENAL TRINITY

My name is Brian Wellman. I currently live in Tennessee. But in September of 2019, I was visiting Moab, Utah, for a vacation with my dad. We were in Canyonlands National Park. I had taken an online night photography class, and I wanted to take some Milky Way photos, so we decided to go out that night and do that.

We had one last night where the moon was going to be down around 10:30 at night, leaving us with a pretty good night sky. It was cloudy and raining in some areas, but it eventually cleared up.

My father was sick that night, and we were trying to decide when we were going to leave. I wanted to sleep a little bit, and then get up at, like, three in the morning and go. But he thought, since he was sick, it would be best to go early in the night, and then he could sleep uninterrupted and hopefully feel better. So we headed out to Canyonlands probably between 9:30 and 10 p.m. I know we got there before the moon was down. I had set up my camera beforehand with all the settings that I needed for some Milky Way photos. I had the camera on a tripod as well.

So we got to the park, and we were looking for a good place to set up where hopefully we wouldn't have any cars or anyone around. So we ended up driving to Shafer Canyon overlook, which is quite a nice overlook towards the east.

As the moon was setting to the west, behind me, I started setting up. I had the tripod pulled out and practiced taking a couple of shots as I waited for the moon to go down. Shortly after it did, I noticed a streak in the sky. I didn't think much of it at first. Probably a shooting star or a meteor. And I went back to getting ready to take some photos.

It was within a minute or so that I saw another streak in the same general area in the sky. So I stopped and looked. That was when I noticed three lights, which I thought looked like they were in formation. I thought to myself... *Wow, that's a UFO!*

So I ran over to my dad. He was sitting in the car again, not feeling well. I told him, "I think we have a UFO out here!" And he actually said to me, "Yeah. I've been watching it out the window. It came over a hill over there!"

So I kept watching this thing. It moved slowly, and then a couple of times, it streaked into a position where it was probably, degree wise from us, 75 degrees or so in the sky.

At that point, I thought it was three different objects. So we watched a little bit longer, and it started to make some incredible movements, streaking through the sky. It was completely silent. It looked like it moved back to where it was before.

Then I looked due east, and there was a very bright, white light in the sky. I told my dad, and once again, he said that he'd seen that, too. At times, he thought it was maybe someone with a flashlight. But he watched it for a while, and it was making really erratic movements. He said he'd actually watched it for quite some time.

So we saw that UFO off to the east, and then we had the one that had come from the southeast. They each had different color lights. The original one had whitish blue lights. Again, at the time, I thought it was three different objects. Then the one that was the bright light to the east looked like one bright white light.

And it was rapidly moving. It looked like a Ping-Pong ball it was moving so fast and erratically down and in and out of the canyons.

It was about this time that I noticed three red lights. They were in the east as well. Again, they looked like something in formation. At one point, they looked like they did a pivot and plunged towards the ground. This really took my breath away because I thought, *Wow... they're going to explode into the ground!* But instead, they just disappeared. There was no sound. No explosion. They were just gone. They would reappear within a few minutes.

At times, there were three different UFOs in the sky all at once. That was when I remembered I had a small pair of binoculars. So I got those out of the car, and I put them on. That was when I could see the original UFO that had come in, and it had stayed pretty much in the same spot. I soon realized that it wasn't three different objects. It was one triangular craft. A black triangle. I gave my dad the binoculars, and we both took a couple of turns looking at it. Just an amazing sight. But it didn't end there.

I took the binoculars back and focused on the bright light towards the east. And when I did, I was stunned. This one that had been bouncing through the canyon was also a triangle! When I then moved my focus to the object with red lights... you guessed it, a third triangle.

I ended up watching these for over two hours. In that time, I captured a few photographs of the white triangle as it was silhouetted on one of the mountains in the distance. These triangles not only made erratic movements, but they were able to streak what looked like miles across the sky in a fraction of a second. They would even look like they disappeared and would appear in another area. At one point, my dad even noticed that the white one that was really bright had pivoted to what looked to be vertical, it turned, and he saw a white light in the center that got really bright, and the triangle seemed to propel itself across the sky.

I didn't really feel any fear during all this. It was amazement. It did feel a bit like we were being surrounded by these triangles at one point. So there was a little bit of apprehension. I knew, at any point, with the sophistication of what we were seeing, that they could do anything they wanted.

Again, my father was sick. So around midnight, we decided to wrap things up and go. The craft were still there, and they were still maneuvering through the canyons and up in the air. I'm not sure what they were doing. I speculate that they were mapping or were doing a reconnaissance of the area. It looked like they were really gathering information about the terrain, or they were looking for something.

I reached out to an author, David Marler, who has written a book about the triangles. I was also featured in the History Channel television series *Unidentified*, in which they did an episode on black triangles. I stayed anonymous at the time, as I was still apprehensive about putting my name out there. But now I realize there's nothing to hide from anymore. I don't mind that people know now.

It was definitely something I will never forget.

Part Two

- CLOSE ENCOUNTERS -

Sightings of strange craft or aerial phenomena is one thing. But coming face-to-face with some sort of being or intelligence that may or may not have to do with said phenomena is a completely different story. The following stories embody that escalation in high strangeness and open the door even wider to glimpse the unknown that lies beyond our understanding.

While we can speculate on the nature of these encounters, and you may even find them much more challenging to accept or believe, they were very real for those involved. Their stories are presented with the same amount of fairness as those who had sightings. These events, no matter what they actually were or weren't, greatly affected those involved. And each individual soon learned that when you stare into the unknown, someone, or some*thing*, will always find a way to stare back.

THE NIGHT VISITOR OF HOLLYWOOD

My name is Michael McMillian. I co-host the *Bigfoot Collectors Club* podcast. This story happened in the early morning of June 29, 2016. Oddly enough, it was just a couple of weeks after I had visited Roswell, New Mexico, of all places.

I live in a ground-floor apartment in Los Angeles. And when I was sleeping one night, I woke up to hearing my bulldog growling from the living room. He was sleeping on the couch, and at first, I thought that he was growling at my neighbor who worked nights at the time. I thought maybe he was coming home, but my dog knows that neighbor very well, and I thought it was odd that he'd be growling. But I could tell, as I sat there for about thirty seconds, listening to his growl get louder, that he was about to start barking. At this point, it was around 4 a.m. I lay there for a moment, when my other dog, a terrier, who was sleeping with me, suddenly shot up, started barking, and ran in to the living room.

I stumbled out of bed, trying to round up the dogs and see what was making them bark. As I turned the corner from my hallway into the living room, I was staring at my window that looks out onto a front porch area. In front of my building, there's a driveway that runs up along the side. That window looks out onto the driveway, where there is small patch of grass with lights that shine upward towards my window. The curtain was drawn, but with the light shining up on the window, I could see the silhouette of a figure.

What was curious about it, though, was instead of it being the silhouette of a human being, the shadow I saw had a long, skinny neck and a rounded head with a pointy chin. I couldn't see any details because the curtains were drawn, but my dogs are going apeshit barking at this thing. And that was when it dawned on me. It was so on the nose that at first I was like, "Well... that looks like an alien!"

It was like a classic gray alien silhouette, something that looked straight out of *Close Encounters of the Third Kind*. As I was looking at it and thinking this, the figure turned its head to its left, which was my right, and I could see the head and neck sort of undulate. I could see where the neck was fused at the back of the head, and it almost looked like a golf wedge.

It was like a classic, gray alien. And when I saw that, I just remember saying, "Holy shit." Looking back, I should have steeled myself, but again, the dogs were going crazy, and it was four o'clock in the morning. So I turned the lights on in my hallway, and this thing ran away from my window towards the back of the building. So I walked down onto my front patio, which overlooks that area. I looked down on my left, and I couldn't see anything at that point.

At this point, my next-door neighbor, the one I thought was originally coming home, he walked out onto his porch, and he asked me what was going on. I didn't want to use the word "alien," so I told him somebody was just looking in my window. And his response gave me chills. He told me, "Oh my gosh... that's so weird because I've been home for an hour, watching Netflix on my laptop in my bedroom, and I kept taking my headphones off because I could have sworn something was in my apartment watching me."

With this, we both walked around the property, but couldn't find anything. That window is about four feet off the ground, and I had my neighbor humor me by asking him to stand outside the window while I went back inside to take a look. He obliged. The silhouette created by my neighbor, who was an average-height male, looked completely different. So what was that silhouette?

Nothing else happened that night, but I did not sleep. There was no other UFO activity that took place. I wasn't experiencing any weird dreams or missing time. There were no lights involved. Nothing of that kind of phenomenon. It was almost as if this... whatever this thing was... was an entity passing by. And I bet, because my bulldog snores so loud, which is often why he's in the living room, I have a feeling this thing was passing through and heard the snoring, and was peering into the window to try to figure out what this sleeping creature was inside this apartment. And then, at some point in the process, my bulldog woke up and sensed that there was something there. And it must have been standing there for a couple of minutes because I was listening to my dog growl at this thing for at least thirty seconds before I got out of bed. So yeah... I don't know what it was. I can only describe it based on what it looked like to me. And what it looked like to me was an alien gray.

I almost have an instinct that this was something that was maybe terrestrial or of this world. Maybe not necessarily of this dimension. I know that sounds weird, but it almost felt like I had seen a leprechaun or an elf more than I had seen an "alien."

Whatever it was, I believe that it was something that was passing by that I was not supposed to see.

TAPPING ON THE WINDOW

This is Brandie from Omaha. Back in October of 2011, my then fiancé and I were driving home from dinner one night. It was still kind of early, so we decided we were going to hit a couple of the local bars on the way home. On our way back, we were coming over this expressway. And as I was looking up, I saw ten reddish, amber-colored lights all throughout the sky.

We really wanted to pull over and just watch, but there was really nowhere on this expressway to pull over safely. So we just kind of slowed down and kept staring and driving. It didn't really seem like any of the other drivers were paying attention to it. Nobody else was slowing down or pulling over or anything. So we were just kind of watching it as we were trying to drive. We just kept noticing more and more of them blinking out there. One of them remained by the time that we got parked to go into one of the bars. I didn't think anything else of it.

A few years later, I had a whirlwind of experiences that all happened at the same time. In April of 2015, I woke to the sound of this tapping noise on what would have been on one window or corner of the house. So I went to go see what was making the noise, and that was when I noticed there was a light outside the window. It was flashing this white and red. It was fascinating. I kept watching, and I noticed that it would bounce and weave and move around. I sat and watched it for maybe about an hour before I just got tired of it and went to bed.

For the next few nights, this light was just there. After about a week or so, I stopped seeing it. After that point, I got hit with this flurry of synchronicities and all kinds of little signs pointing to things that were going on in my life. I had this mad rush to try to take in and consume anything I could about UFOs, aliens, and anything of that fashion. It was just a nonstop drive to consume everything that I could.

At this time, a lot of childhood memories came back of stuff that had happened to me, collectively, over the years. This included one experience that I always thought was a dream, but now thinking back, I don't think that was the case.

I lived right next to my grandparents when I was younger. So during the summer when my parents were at work, I had free rein to bounce between my grandma's house and mine. And this one summer afternoon, I was playing in my room. My room had four windows because it was on the back corner of the house. They were pretty high, too. About ten feet off the ground or so.

So I had this girl come and tap at my window. I didn't think anything of it at first because I had half sisters who would sometimes come and visit me. So I thought maybe it was one of them. I remember her coming to play with me one other time. She had red hair. And for some reason, I thought she was another one of my half sisters because I only saw her a couple of times. Mind you, I was pretty young, four or five years old. I didn't really pay attention to who some of these people were. And this girl, she came tapping at my window, and I remember thinking, *How did she get up there?*

She wanted me to come outside and play. So I did. We were playing on the swing set. I kept asking, "How did you get up to the window?" She pointed to a piece of metal that was up against the side of the house and told me she climbed up it. I remember trying to climb it myself to get to the window, and I couldn't. I kind of blew it off at the time, and a little later while we were playing, she kept trying to ask me to do something. I don't remember what the question was, but I was just so distraught. I remember thinking, *You're mean! I don't want you to come and play with me anymore!* But she kept trying to convince me to go somewhere with her, and I didn't want to go with her. Then the next thing I remember, I was standing in the backyard, and behind my bedroom, there was a fenced-off garden. In this garden was this little ship thing. And I remember she was trying to get me to go inside the ship. I was telling her I didn't want to, and I was pleading with her to not make me go inside. She got really mean and pushy.

I don't remember ever actually going inside, but I do remember being inside it. I remember being on this dark table. The room was dark, but it had this weird amber kind of lighting against the floor. Instead of being faceup on this table, I was facedown, and I remember being told not to look. At that point, I went from being upset to just angry. This girl was talking to whoever was behind me, and I wasn't allowed to look. I was mad about it, and I remember just lying there, crying and crying.

The next thing I knew, I was back in bed in my room and just sobbing. I remember just having such relief, thinking it was all just a terrible dream. But after that, I remember having friends over, and I remember showing them where this girl said she'd climbed up to the window. We all tried to do it, and none of us could.

Thinking back, it wasn't a dream. It really did happen. That experience with the girl was a major wake-up call for me. I've had a lot of mornings where I've had weird dreams, where I felt like someone was in the room with me. I've woken up with marks to correspond with the kinds of dreams I've had.

In some way, I was kind of happy that I had some sort of justification for all the weird things that have happened my entire life. But it was also very alarming because I have no control over it. It's kind of lonesome because you don't really have anybody you can talk to about it. Thankfully, my dad has kind of had similar experiences, so he has been my saving grace in that I can talk to him about some of the goings-on in my life. We've even had a few shared events. So that's been nice. But for the most part, it's opened my eyes to a lot of things, and it's made me appreciate and take great value in life. To have a whole new outlook on humanity.

It's also very stressful, though. Because you never know when things are going to flare up again. And you have no control of how it's going to affect your life outwardly. A lot of times, you just want to talk to somebody about it, but you don't always have that opportunity. So you're struggling with things in your private life that you can't really explain to anybody else.

My experiences have taught me to have a really good balancing act in life. It's also taught me that we're not the only people who experience things like this. So in many different ways, we are never truly alone.

THE MANTIS MAN

My name is Patrick McFadden. In 1996, I had a UFO sighting that pretty much blew the doors off my reality. It took place in Montana, and the story leading up to the sighting is almost just as good as the sighting itself.

I was twenty years old at the time. I worked very hard for a baseball scholarship. But that was taken away from me. But instead of wallowing in self-pity, I convinced a friend of mine to move. When I left high school, most of the guys were going to either Colorado or Arizona. And I said, you know, let's change this up. So my buddy and I moved to Montana.

During our first month there, it was in the middle of winter. We were sitting in an empty apartment for a month, knew nobody, and then this guy Todd just started knocking on our door all the time. He was absolutely nuts. We knew it. But we had nothing to do, so we would let him come in and hang out.

So Todd started showing up every day, sitting in our living room, and just spewing conspiracy theories. Telling us that December 31, 1999, was going to be the end of the world and that we should get ready. Or that AIDS and cancer were mainlined into society by the American government. Just the most ridiculous stuff. But I was a twenty-year-old kid, and this was entertaining. So we'd just sit there and listen to him.

Todd would always bring up this cabin he owned up in the north part of Montana, and this was where he was going to get ready for "Y2K." Where he and these people in his commune were going prepare for the end of the world. So we listened to him for about a month straight, spewing this nonsense. And then, one day, he asked us if we wanted to see the cabin. We said yes.

Now, Montana is a big state. So it was a long drive. But we were bored, and we jumped in my car one night, and we started driving with Todd. He ended up giving us some wrong directions, and we got stuck in the snow. We were not going anywhere, so we had to start walking. And we started walking through the Montana wilderness in the middle of winter, with somebody we knew was certifiably crazy. And he just kept telling us, "This is the way to my cabin... if we don't make it to my cabin, we're gonna freeze to death. So your car's stuck, you're going nowhere, and if you don't follow me, you're dead." So... we really had no choice. We followed him.

So we got off the road, and we started walking through the woods. Todd was still firing off these conspiracy theories. We were just afraid for our lives, so as we were walking through the woods, we were starting to give up hope. And then he pointed to something ahead of us. It was a clearing in the woods!

So Todd gathered his bearings, and we were waiting to find out if we were still lost or not. At this point, it was about three in the morning, and we were under a pitch-black, perfectly clear Montana sky. Even in this possibly life-threatening situation, I couldn't help but appreciate the beautiful sky above. But then reality set back in.

As we continued trudging through the snow, Todd was still not sure where we were. And he continued to spout all his conspiracy theories. We weren't saying a word, and he finally turned back to us and said, "You don't believe me. You don't believe anything I'm telling you!"

At this point, my friend and I were getting pretty angry. And I couldn't take it anymore. I just shouted to him, "Just shut the fuck up and get us to your cabin!"

Todd just stood there, looking towards us. Not at us. But towards us. And I wasn't quite sure what to expect next. Was he gonna leave us there? Or worse, was he gonna kill us?

And he just said, "We're not going anywhere until you tell me what that is."

He pointed up to the sky, and reluctantly, my friend and I looked up. And there it was. The size of a full moon. But it wasn't the moon. I could see the moon. This thing was... it was circular. It was piercing white on top and green on the bottom, with this red strobe going across it. Just pulsating across.

My friend and I looked up, and we saw this thing. Immediately, we just fell back in the snow, amazed. Granted, the snow was like three feet high anyways. But still. We just fell over, lay there, and we were looking at this thing. It wasn't moving at all.

I remember looking at Todd. And he almost looked bored. Like he'd seen this thing a million times before. But we just lay there for about a minute. And then all of a sudden, this thing just started dancing all over the place. This thing went from just hanging over our heads to, within a split second, dancing up and around the Rocky Mountain peaks. It would then come to a quick rest, and it would stop for a few seconds. Then it would just start dancing above the peaks again.

I remember looking over at my friend, and he literally had tears streaming down the sides of his face. It made me cry, too. It was like a combination of terror and awe, and we didn't even know what to think.

Todd was standing right next to us the whole time, watching. He said to us, "There's usually four or five of those things all flying around in formation. That's why my wife and my daughter won't come back up here anymore. They're too scared."

We kept watching. Todd then told us, "Wait till you meet my friends tomorrow. They'll tell you stories about these things that you won't believe."

We ended up making it to Todd's cabin that night. Alive. The next morning, we met one of his friends, who told us about a run-in they had with these lighted objects when they were hunting near Todd's cabin. They said it was a circular craft. Metallic. Basically a flying saucer. It floated over the trees, just above treetop level, and this guy and his friend were just watching this thing. And that was when, in my opinion, these guys made a bad decision.

One of these guys... he took a shot at this thing! It wasn't too far away. He said it was maybe a hundred feet off the ground. And this guy took a shot at it. He said he didn't know if he hit it, but he said that the craft actually buckled after he shot. It actually started moving toward him.

So they ran for cover in the tree line. Then this craft slowly started to move over the trees and started following them. So while they were in the trees, the craft pretty much was trying to find them. This guy then told me that at the very last moment the craft found them, they were pretty much hugging a tree, just trying not to be seen or heard. That was when he saw the bottom of the craft open up.

He told me that when it opened up, it spilled this gelatinous, red liquid, and it got all over them. He then told me that the other guy, about a year and a half after this, was riddled with tumors all over his body where this liquid had spilled on him. Whatever this stuff was, if it wasn't radioactive, it was extremely poisonous.

So between Todd and this guy, I asked them what they thought these things were. Like, did they think these things weren't from here. Again, all these guys were conspiracy theorists through and through. Again, they were getting ready for the end of the world. So with this stuff, they thought it was the American government. No other culprit than the big bad government. Even if a straight-up alien just came up and looked at them in the face, they would still think it was the American government.

We ended up leaving there later that day to get our car and make our way out of the woods and back home safely.

They call Montana "Big Sky Country" for a reason. It's just black. And if you ask anybody in Montana, I would say one out of five people will tell you a great UFO story. And this was the story that started it all for me.

The next story I have is completely different. The best way to fully understand exactly what I saw and experienced late one night back in 2014, we have to go back to 2011 to what a very good friend of mine saw in the same exact location in the northwest corner of New Jersey in a rural area on the Musconetcong River.

My friend Mark is a very prominent businessman and upstanding member of the community. So when he talks, people tend to listen. And when he dropped this story on me one day, I was shell-shocked to say the least. He had kept it bottled up for almost three years and finally unloaded it, for the first time, on me.

So again, back in 2011, he and his brother were fishing one day on the river. They both had hip waders on at the time. So they were standing in the water, and they kept hearing this high whizzing sound. He and his brother just kept looking at each other, not knowing what to make of it. After a few minutes, he had the compulsion to look to his right. And that was when he saw it.

Standing there in the water, right next to him, was this half mantis, half man. Almost eight feet tall. He said it was way more insect-like than it looked like a man, but it had the physical maneuvers and the motor functions of a human. This thing was looming over him. He said he couldn't believe what he was looking at, obviously. But he also said in the first couple of moments, he felt that this thing couldn't believe that it was actually being seen!

Mark immediately fell back into the water out of pure fright. He said as he was looking at it, it was looking back at him. And that it was peering deep into his soul and that it was very overwhelming. He didn't feel any evil coming from it, and it felt like what he believed it would have been like looking at God.

This entire experience, he said, lasted for all of fifteen seconds. Suddenly, there was this body-length halo around the Mantis Man. This orange light. And then almost instantly, the Mantis Man completely disappeared.

After it disappeared, he looked to his brother, and he could tell immediately that his brother had seen it as well. The brother left Mark there, trying to claw his way out of the water. Mark eventually made it back to the car and tried to contact his brother, but he was long gone by then.

Since that day, the brothers barely speak. And every time Mark has tried to bring it up, the brother refuses to talk about it.

So this brings us to 2014. I found myself almost in the same exact location where Mark's experience had taken place. I took my dog for a walk one night, and we went into an old abandoned campground that was right there. I decided to cut off the trail and walk into the woods a little bit.

As I was walking with the dog, I started looking into the woods. That was when I saw this very bright orange orb, about fifty or so yards away. At first I thought maybe it was a garage light or something. But I knew the area pretty well and realized there were no houses or anything back there. It definitely wasn't somebody with a flashlight, either, because this orange light kept going from the forest floor up into the trees. Then it would come back down. Just moving up and down over and over again.

The forest floor was very flat, so I sat there with the dog and just looked at this thing. As I was looking at it, I could tell it was moving a little closer and getting brighter. It was a very weird orange. It would go from dark to light, almost like it was refracting light and then turning it into these different bright and dark orange colors. The other thing that I found very strange was that the entire forest was completely quiet. Not a single sound of animals, insects, or even the wind. Dead silent.

As I was noticing the complete lack of noise, the most incredible thing happened. Every four-legged animal in the woods just went blowing by me on both sides of my periphery. Deer, rabbits, and a bunch of other creatures. They were all around me and my dog. My dog wasn't even on her feet when this happened. She was just lying there, trembling. And when I looked back and caught focus of this orange light, I noticed it was still moving towards me at a more rapid pace now. I was petrified.

I eventually got to my feet. And without my dog even getting up, I just dragged her out of the woods to where the road of the campground was. I looked back, and I saw that the orange light started moving right to where I was sitting. As I stood there, with all the hair on my body standing up, I watched this orange light go from just hovering in the woods to shooting straight up through the canopy of the trees and disappearing out of sight.

I contacted Mark and told him about this. We had gotten together many times after that to do nothing but discuss my event and his. We used to get together maybe once every two weeks. Then it was, like, twice a week. I basically became like a therapist for him. He would just recount the story over and over again, and we would break it apart. So I told him one day, "Let me look up if anybody else has seen this thing on the river." And to our surprise, there's a guy who wasn't far away who made an entire website on the Mantis Man of the Musconetcong River!

Apparently, this thing has been seen multiple times by different people. But this guy... what he said would resonate with Mark and gave me chills. He told us that when he saw the Mantis

Man, it was completely enveloped in a light and then disappeared. He described it, just as Mark had, like looking at God.

I would eventually write a little article about this and put it online in a local forum. And just by chance, some Discovery Channel TV show found it and asked me if I would contact Mark so they could interview him. Mark agreed, as long as he remained anonymous. And what I always respected about Mark is that he never wavered from his story. Not one bit.

Mark once told me he wished he'd never seen the Mantis Man. But, in finally telling his story, and knowing I, and many others, had strange experiences in the same vicinity, it was a type of closure for him and for me, too.

No matter what these experiences were or weren't, there is something truly bizarre and profound happening in the northwest corner of New Jersey. Particularly around the Musconetcong River.

ALIEN ON THE SIDEWALK

My name is Michael Koslow. My first experience occurred back in 1993 when I was living in a suburb of Northern New Jersey. I was twenty years old at the time. It was a rainy evening, and I was driving west towards my home with one of my close friends in the passenger seat beside me. We drove up a long drawn-out hill, and as we arrived at the peak, I noticed a bright yet strangely reserved pair of lights not too far off in the distance straight ahead of us. I say reserved because, to me, they seemed bright, but were more softly glowing like the moon.

This particular road stretched for several miles between two towns and was flanked by low, swampy grasslands on either side of the road. The lights were side by side and resembled the headlights of a vehicle except that they were not on the road but rather they were slightly above it. They did not appear to be moving. My friend later estimated that the lights were approximately twenty-five feet straight above the pavement. It seemed peculiar to me, so I brought it to my friend's attention. He acknowledged that he was already aware of it. There were no cell phones at the time, and we did not have a camera with us. However, my friend happened to be carrying a small tape recorder with a cassette tape. So he pressed the record button and began to describe what we were seeing.

As we approached the bizarre lights, it became more and more apparent that this was not an airplane or a helicopter. There was no civilian drone technology at the time, either. We confirmed that the lights were stationary, as they remained in the same position, yet appeared to increase in size as we got closer to them.

Just as we were about to drive underneath them, one of the lights lifted quickly, while remaining equidistant from the other. And the two, which now appeared to be part of a single object that neither of us could make out, shot off to the north and disappeared instantly in the snap of a finger. Poof. Gone. Just like that. Although we were unable to capture any photos, an audio recording of our emotional response to the event is evidence that the two of us witnessed something. Shocking enough to cause us both to yell out, "Holy shit!" in our shared state of astonishment and wonder.

I remember that the two of us were hysterical, and tears were streaming down our faces. To my knowledge, this has never happened to either one of us before while witnessing an airplane or a helicopter. I would also like to mention that whatever this thing was, it was completely silent.

My friend wrote the following in his diary entry on this day:

When we were in the car, we were contending with driving sounds. Engine, tires on road, and the rain adds quite a bit to clatter. However, there is no question we were very close to the source of light, and at no point had I even considered that I didn't hear anything usual or unusual. I can't buy into a scenario where we transect a small engine plane's flight path or big private jet. It was definitely not a helicopter, as they are a lot louder than planes, and they disturb everything around with turbulent rotors.

When this occurred, we were about a mile or so away from my apartment. So we continued to rave about our experience with the tape recorder still running. There were other vehicles on the road as well. Did anybody else see this?

This is where and when the high strangeness really peaked. As we approached our destination, my friend shut off the tape recorder, and we drove a short distance, entranced in complete silence. Suddenly, I observed one of the most odd things that I had ever seen in my life.

Casually walking down the sidewalk just around the corner from my home was what appeared to be a stereotypical gray alien. Slender and lanky, with long thin, wiry arms, legs and fingers. It had a large bulbous head with big dark eyes. I couldn't believe what I was looking at! Was anybody else seeing this? There were other cars on the road here as well and people coming and going relatively nearby.

Before I could say anything to my friend, he uttered with a bewildered tone to his voice, "Did you see that?" I said something to the effect of, "The thing with the big head walking down the sidewalk?" He nervously responded, "Yes."

We both fell silent again and drove the rest of the way to my place, where we spent the remainder of the evening calmly discussing all that had happened to us. For some odd reason, my friend is unable to recall this last part of the experience, with the appearance of the alien being on the sidewalk. Although he recalls everything else with as much clarity as I do. And with nearly identical descriptions of the phenomena as those of my own.

I'd like to share some thoughts as to what some of the possibilities are in regard to what these phenomena could potentially be. All, of course, are entirely speculative. It could be extraterrestrial. Perhaps even as some speculate, interdimensional. I have experienced peculiar geometric craft and extremely vivid dreams. I have woken up from lucid dreams with the thought that these are some sort of reality-bending craft from liminal worlds that seem to have a being or consciousness of their own. Perhaps biological. Perhaps artificial intelligence. Perhaps some sort of hybrid of the two. Their very presence seems to warp reality or consciousness.

Perhaps they are dream states. Or hallucinations. Psychedelic spaces or a myriad of other states of awareness all blending together in various ways into incomprehensible hyperspaces that seem to profoundly transform the human experience of sensation and perception. Perhaps it is human or nonhuman time travelers. Perhaps it is highly advanced human technology from the past or future. Perhaps it is human-generated artificial intelligence. Perhaps it is a biological creature or creatures that coexist on our planet that are technologically more advanced than we are. Perhaps it is from the depths of our deserts or the depths of our oceans. Perhaps it is from the depths of our jungles.

Maybe the phenomenon is holographic. Maybe the phenomenon is the hallucination of a mass psychosis or mass hypnosis. Maybe the phenomenon is a mind virus. Maybe the phenomenon is a hoax. Maybe the phenomenon is a Tulpa or thought formation created consciously or subconsciously by individuals or collectively that takes on a life of its own apart from its generator or generators. Maybe the phenomena are what many through the ages have commonly been referred to as angels, demons, or fairies, or elves.

Are they some sort of probes observing life on our planet? Are humans some sort of genetic experiment? Could the so-called "zoo hypothesis" be correct? Are they somehow associated with death in the after-death state?

Anyone's guess is as good as mine on all of these. The only thing I know for sure is that something out of the ordinary and perhaps out of this world happened to my friend and me in 1993. Memory changes over time. And although it is within the range of possibility that the explanation for the experience is entirely prosaic, I cannot shake this deeply rooted feeling that this is not the case.

Part Three

- MILITARY INCIDENTS -

The final stories we will explore all took place directly on or around military installations, stations, and bases. They were witnessed and experienced by active-duty personnel who either reported what they had seen and encountered, or for fear of ridicule, or even losing their careers, chose not to report the event.

While the stigma behind reporting such sightings and encounters is shedding, this clearly was not the case when many of these events occurred. Those who did report were told not to speak publicly about the events, presumably either for classified reasons, or simply another case of stigma and ridicule feared within their ranks.

These events highlight a troubling gap in the security above and around these highly sensitive areas. These events also highlight the fact that the witnesses are, by all means, trained observers. And even with those skills in full effect, these individuals still could not explain what they had seen and experienced.

And like many in the civilian world, these events had and have lasting effects, sometime traumatic, on those involved.

The author wishes to thank these individuals, specifically, for their service to their respective military branches, and also for having the courage to come forward during and after their service.

THE NAVAL STATION INVASION

My name is Angelo Accetta. I served in the United States Navy from 2009 to 2013. During my time, I served as an aviation maintenance administrator, working logistics for the F-18 Super Hornet fighter jets, and was stationed for shore duty at FRC West at Lemoore Naval Air Station, in Lemoore, California. From 2011 to 2012, while on duty, I witnessed multiple sightings of what I believe to have been the same UFO on five different occasions. These are my sightings.

The first sighting occurred on November 15, 2011, at approximately 11:30 p.m. I was on watch duty from 8 p.m. to midnight. As I was walking back towards my post from the enlisted barracks E building, I noticed an object in the night sky.

This object was too slow to be an F-18 Super Hornet, which I am very familiar with due to my job. I then realized it was not shaped like a jet. It had a triangular look to it, with lights glowing below it. The distance from my point of view was at least five hundred yards away, and it was moving away from the airstrip, which was only few miles down the road. For me to see it and acknowledge the shape and size, I'd say it was about three thousand to five thousand feet above. But its speed and how smooth it seemed to be moving, almost like it was gliding on water. I was memorized by what I was seeing. After about three minutes of the object going in the same direction, it suddenly shot off at immeasurable speed and disappeared out of sight.

Later that morning, I contacted my superior and informed them of what I had witnessed. They immediately laughed and jokingly asked if I had been drinking on the job. This response was all I needed to remain quiet. I was fresh out of basic at my first command, and I did not want my superior officers and other shipmates to look at me differently. Word travels fast on military bases, and I didn't want to be labeled a weirdo or crackpot. But then it happened again.

My second sighting happened on December 24, 2011, at approximately 9 p.m. Walking to my car from my barracks, just as I was about to get into my car, I looked up to my right, and I noticed the same triangular flying object again. This time much closer than before. It was moving at around the same speed. This time, I just stood next to my car door and watched it as it went from right to left and disappeared in distance. In my opinion, it almost seemed as if it was doing some sort of recon mission.

The third event occurred on February 3, 2012, at approximately 2 a.m. I was on watch duty again. But this time, I had a shipmate with me. We were walking towards barracks D, smoking cigarettes. He blew smoke up into the air, and he noticed something in the sky, moving far too slowly to be our F-18s. It was, in fact, the triangle again. I was waiting for him to say something, but it was like he was memorized, like I had been. I was thrilled that somebody else was actually here to witness this with me!

We both watched as the triangle stopped. It was far lower to the ground than the previous events. Maybe two thousand feet. Then, like a golf ball being hit, it shot off into the sky and disappeared. After this thing was gone, I asked him what he thought it could be. All he could say was that he didn't think it was from "here."

After this event, having had another witness, I told him we should report it. But he refused. The stigma and ridicule was too heavy a possibility for him to bear. I left that night excited, but also feeling pretty upset that this kept happening and nobody was reporting it or doing anything about it.

The fourth event happened on June 11, 2012, at approximately 11:30 p.m. Driving on base from work, there is one long road that goes straight from the center of the base to the airstrip and workstations. It's about a seven-mile, straight long road. As I was driving, I noticed the same object ahead of me in the sky off to my left. This time was crazy because I knew some squadrons were doing night mission practice ops. I couldn't believe that there was not one F-18 in the sky during the time this object was in our airspace! This time it actually went over my head and behind me. That was when I lost sight of it.

My fifth sighting of the triangle happened on October 12, 2012, at approximately 1 a.m. This was my last sighting of the object until my departure from NAS Lemoore. I was on night watch duty, on the roof of barracks E. In the distance, I saw the object again. At this point, I was furious with myself and with the object. I was furious that nobody else had reported it, or maybe this was one of our own new jets or something and nobody had informed us. But I just stared up at it one last time, wanting with all my pent-up curiosity and anger to just scream, "Show yourselves! Come closer!"

At the time, I just hated seeing something with my own eyes, multiple times, and not being able to speak about it without being asked if I was drinking or having my corroborating witness not want to talk about it either. That night, I walked away from the sight of the object and went about my night detail.

After hearing the recent accounts of Navy pilots and personnel talking about their own UFO sightings, that was when I finally felt comfortable enough telling my story. I just had the birth of my first child. As her father, I want her to grow up realizing that we are not alone in this universe, and one day, whoever they are, they'll present themselves to us.

If there's one thing I can end with, it's to not be afraid of telling your story. Nobody will persecute you or think you're crazy anymore. Thousands of people have witnessed what I witnessed, all around the world. I will never forget those sightings.

Every single day when I wake up, I always look into the sky, wondering if they'll visit again.

INCIDENT AT CFB GAGETOWN

M y name is David Marceau. I am a senior manager for a major corporation in the United States. When I was nineteen years old, I had a close encounter with a UFO on a military base in 1992.

What I saw wasn't your typical sighting. A lot of UFO sightings seem to be some strange lights in the sky. Things you really can't identify, which is why we call them unidentified flying objects. What I saw wasn't unidentified. I knew right away what I was looking at. It was unmistakable.

At the time, I was in the woods, in military service. I was an Army reservist, and my unit was doing our annual summer training up at Gagetown military base in New Brunswick, Canada. We were an ammo unit, so even though my specialty was not ammunition, everyone had to pull guard duty. It was the second week of August 1992. I had to go out at 11 p.m. one night. I had to guard an enormous pile of ammunition out in the woods. There were three sites, three of us each guarding a site. This night, I and another guard (we'll call him Mike) witnessed something in the sky.

Around 11:20 p.m., I looked at about my one o'clock position from where I was sitting. And over the tree line was an enormous spaceship. I've been criticized for jumping to that conclusion, but I can't apologize for that. All I can say is that it was a spaceship. It was there in front of me, no less than a hundred yards away.

Later, I would be interviewed by former Pentagon UFO program director Luis Elizondo about the incident. I would be featured on the History Channel television series *Unidentified* about the event. During the interview, Elizondo would refer to me as a "trained observer." At the time, I'd never heard that term before, but as soon as he said it, that made sense for me. I actually was trained at the time. We had these flash cards that were like playing cards. And each of them had a silhouette of an aircraft. It was either a NATO or Soviet aircraft, and we were taught to identify them by their shape. So that if it was dark or if they were far away, we would know whether to shoot them or not.

In reference to the craft itself, since I was in a one-acre clearing, I have always estimated it could have been well over one hundred feet long and as much as fifty feet high. It's hard to say for sure, but it was close to me, and it was enormous. The shape was like a somewhat flattened egg, which had a slight apex just behind the nose and tapered off towards the tail. The nose and tail were more flat, and the transition from top/bottom to front/back had a slight edge.

It was a gun-metal gray, not completely dull but no shine. No seams or rivets, and completely smooth. No markings of any type. No lights except for the three at the front of the ship, which covered about a 120-degree arc across the front. This was what allowed Mike, the other witness, to see what he thought was a flare, which never fell to the ground. The lights are what have always fascinated me the most.

I still don't know for sure if they were headlights or windows. I suppose I never will. If you had asked me thirty years ago, I would have leaned towards windows because we did not have drones in the military in the early '90s. When they were eventually used in combat, they were significantly smaller than this thing and had wings and engines. And they make noise and cannot hover or move at less than one mile per hour.

The craft made absolutely no noise as it passed over and disappeared out of sight. Once the ship got a certain distance away from me, I heard a slight staticky sound, like a TV with nothing tuned in. Interestingly, nothing around me made any noise when this thing approached. And for years, I thought this was because the crickets, frogs, and all the nighttime critters knew something. Some kind of instinct and they were all quiet because there was some danger there. But more recently, I've come to the conclusion that the ship may have had some type of noise-cancellation technology, and that's why everything around me was silent.

For full disclosure, my sighting was featured on an episode of the History Channel television series *Unidentified: Inside America's UFO Investigation*. In the episode I was featured on, they included a clip of me mentioning that static sound. But they edited out the fact that I did not hear static the whole time. I heard nothing. It was only after the ship got a ways away from me that I heard the static, and then it was only briefly. I have thought for some time that this was an effect that was due to the noise-cancellation device traveling out of range, causing sound to return. This is based on having grown up near an airbase and witnessing F-16s coming out of hypersonic flight. The sound catches up to them with a sucking "whoosh" sound. It's pretty cool. This would be sort of the opposite of that. Perhaps someday in our lifetimes, someone will invent a noise-cancellation device like this and we can all experience it firsthand.

I also have a third theory on the silence, these days. A couple of times in my life, I have experienced stress combined with what I believe is consuming too much sodium, which caused my blood pressure to get jacked up. This then caused a pounding in my ears, making it difficult to hear momentarily. It could be that the terror

I felt during the incident caused my blood pressure to increase to the extent that it drowned out all sound around me. That doesn't explain the static later, but it could explain the lack of sound from the wildlife in the woods. It's also a much more mundane explanation than the other two, and not as fun to think about, but it's a possibility.

This event was terrifying. It was the most traumatic thing that's ever happened to me. I was literally scared stiff. I've done a lot of small-game hunting, and I remember when my dad was teaching me to hunt, he would tell me that if we were to come up on a pheasant, it isn't going to fly away until after we've passed it. This is because they know that they fly too slowly, and if they try to fly out in front of you, then they'll get shot. But they'll let you go by, and then they fly out behind you. Then they can get away. Sometimes people even step on them because they're not going to move. And I was in that mode when this thing was coming by, traveling probably less than a mile an hour. It may have been hovering motionless at first. It's hard to remember. But this was about a five-minute encounter.

Beyond that, I kept watching it, but while it was in my vicinity, I couldn't move. I suppose I could have, but I was trying not to because I didn't want to be seen. At the time, there was no drone technology like we have now. So the thought that the thing might be unmanned was not even a possibility. So I assumed there was something inside piloting the thing. And that if I moved, it or they would see me. Then every science fiction show and movie that I had ever seen started going through my head. I thought maybe they'd beam me up, or they'd zap me with a death ray or something, and I'd disappear, and no one would ever know what happened to me! All of this was going through my head at the time. I was just terrified, not moving, just following this ship with my eyes, enough to keep it in sight until it was, uh, uh, leaving my field of vision. It was at that point that I had to get up and kind of follow it, because I was afraid that it might circle back around and over me.

The whole encounter lasted about five to seven minutes. I finally did start talking about it. Initially, the other guy who saw it a few sites away, we told everyone in our unit about it, and then we got ridiculed. We were the laughingstocks and lost all credibility. So we stopped talking about it. And then after that, I don't think I told anyone for about another five years or so.

I think it was in the late '90s when I told my cousin and his wife about it. At that time, it was like I had been transported back to that moment and started reliving the terror of the incident. My eyes welled up. I didn't actually shed a tear, but my eyes were as full of water as they could be. Because of the ridicule that I had faced years earlier when this thing happened, I asked my cousin's girlfriend (later, his wife), "Do you believe me?" and she said, "Well, I can see you're visibly shaking." And she was right. I had physical symptoms of the trauma from that night.

So after I finally told them, and they believed me, it was a little bit easier to start telling people. I still didn't tell everyone I met, because I didn't want people to think I was a weirdo. But little by little, I started to let the cat out of the bag. Early on in my relationship with my wife, I let her know about it, and she was cool with it. And it ended up being this open secret within my extended family. And that was when my sister-in-law actually ended up sending me that 2017 *New York Times* article about the Pentagon UFO program and the former director Luis Elizondo.

I eventually was able to track Elizondo down, and that led to me telling my story on *Unidentified*. One thing that Elizondo asked me was, "How has this changed you?" And I said at the time that this event has made me fearless, in a sense. I feel fear, but I don't feel it in the way that I would have before this incident. What I can liken it to is how if you've ever smoked a cigarette or drank a beer. That first cigarette or drink gets you really high or drunk. But once you've had more and more as time goes on, you don't feel it as much. So someone who's been drinking for ten years can still get drunk, but not off of one beer. That's what fear is like for me now. I still feel it, but it doesn't affect me as much.

No words can really describe the terror that I felt when an alien spaceship was no less than a hundred yards from me. I was out in the middle of the woods in who knows where in Canada. I was armed with an M16 rifle, but no bullets. There had been an incident a few years back where civilians had stolen some ammunition, and some American soldiers shot at them. So this time around, in order to avoid an international incident, they sent us out there with our weapons, but no ammunition. It was just for show.

So I don't know whoever was flying that ship, if they could see that I was armed and possibly a threat, but not know that I didn't actually have any ammunition in the weapon... so I really wasn't a threat. I felt like a sitting duck out there. It was extraordinarily terrifying.

So that's my story. And I'm sticking with it.

THE CRATE IN THE DESERT

M y name is Jeremy McGowan. When I was twenty years old, I decided to join the United States Air Force. After basic training, I was enrolled in Security Police Technical School and was assigned to Pope Air Force Base in North Carolina. This was right when Desert Storm had started, so after only a few weeks, I was deployed to the Middle East. The vast majority of my time was spent at the rank of E5, which is a staff sergeant. I spent a grand total of two and a half years combined time in the Middle East. I was also attached with Joint Special Operations Command (JSOC). I did about two years down in South America with about a year being in Panama and a year deep in the jungles of Colombia, doing counter narcotics operations and things like that.

At the end of my first four years, I decided to move from active duty to the USAF Reserves. But in 1995, I was given the opportunity to go back to the Middle East.

To paint a backdrop to everything I'm going to reveal here, only four years earlier, the Soviet Union had collapsed, and we saw the formation of nation-states, and we saw countries being born from the rubble. These countries didn't have a political history and had become brand-new entities. And a lot of those entities had nuclear weapons, because the Soviet Union had placed nuclear weapons throughout their entire territory. So now you had these nation-states or countries with not only new parliaments and new militaries, but their own nuclear weapons. And this will play heavily into my story.

So at Pope Air Force Base, where I was set to deploy from, we were always accustomed to getting strange deployments and very little notice. But usually, they were just for training. But this one was interesting. There was me and nine other people. We were told to pack a bag and get on a plane. We had no idea where we were going or why.

We initially flew to Dover Air Force Base in Delaware and transferred aircraft to a C-5 Galaxy. Climbing into the aircraft with the other nine of my team, I noticed that we weren't alone. Already on the aircraft were several dozen very somber-looking folks in a variety of desert camouflage uniforms. Being stationed at Pope AFB, I was very accustomed to the special ops in uniform. Pope was in the center of Fort Bragg and maintained training for Rangers, SEALs, Green Berets, and JSOC. Being attached to JSOC support, I'd deployed with some of them before. But this was different. They wouldn't even look at us as we found our seats and stowed our gear. The flight crew wouldn't talk to us, either. It was all just very different.

It wasn't until we were airborne and past the point of no return that we were told we were heading to Jordan. At this point, I'd been in the military for a few years and served a significant amount of time in the Middle East. But nothing ever happened in Jordan. So this definitely made me curious.

The flight seemed like it had lasted a lifetime. While in the cargo bay, I could see a lot of the equipment that had been loaded. There were JSOC dune buggies, weapons crates, pallets of bottled water, and an extraordinary amount of satellite communication gear. This felt less and less like a mobility exercise and more like a well-coordinated and planned operation. But for what, I still had no idea.

When we landed, the first thing I noticed was that we were on a Jordanian air base that looked like it had been demolished. It was in the worst state of repair of any place I'd ever seen. Then I found myself in our first briefing. This was when we were told that we were now participating in Operation Ellipse Foxtrot, a joint services exercise. My team would be tasked with the security of various depots and remote sites supporting this exercise. But this was no exercise. This was a full-blown operation in Jordan. Yet I had no idea why or for how long.

Days went by with no marching orders. Then, all of a sudden, my team just sat around with no marching orders. And then, all of a sudden, we all got split up. This never happens. Staying together is paramount to combat survival, and splitting up a team is just something that isn't done. But it was done. To this day, I don't know where the rest of my team went or what their duties were. But I definitely remember mine.

I was issued 240 rounds of ammunition for my M16 and given 18 rounds of HEDP grenades for the M203. I was then transported to my post. I would be working a graveyard shift of security, which I liked, because it was a lot cooler at night in the desert. This post was a significant distance into the desert. There was nothing but sand, some rocks, a few dunes, and some tire tracks for as far as the eye could see. Then a sizable beige tent appeared in the middle of the desert. I was stopped a few dozen meters before the tent and told that this was my post and that I'd be there for several days. There was a latrine, a pallet of water, MREs, the tent, and one other USAF Security Police Officer whom I did not recognize.

From out of the tent came a captain (or possibly a major, I can't remember), and he walked us around the side of the tent and showed us an enormous wooden crate. Large enough to house a car. It had no markings, placards, or any identifiers of what its contents could be.

This superior told us, "This is your priority. Don't get near the crate. Don't let anyone else get near it."

Naturally, I asked what was in the crate.

"Don't ask that question," I was told.

And that was pretty much it. There were no written standard operation protocols, no rules of engagement, no maps, nothing. Just the order to not get near it and not let anyone else get near it. I pushed one more time and asked, "Sir, what do we do if someone does get near the crate?"

His reply was blunt: "Shoot them."

So for three nights, that was what I did. I just walked around and guarded this giant crate in the desert.

During the day, a truck would come, pick us up, take us to the mess hall for chow, and then we'd go to our quarters, get a shower, sleep, and do it again the next night. It was in the mess hall when something else really got me curious about what was going on here. When I looked around, I noticed there were people from the Army Rangers, Naval Special Warfare, different command staff, and even personnel from the FBI. But the thing that really stood out to me was that there was also a handful of individuals from the US Department of Energy. Everyone else, well, I'd seen their kind and served with them on other deployments throughout the Middle East. But never had I seen anyone from the DoE. Something important was definitely going on around this base in the desert.

Guarding the crate was fairly easy, to be honest. Because there wasn't a single other person out there but me and the other security officer. And since nobody was really monitoring us at the time, we both just did our own thing. It was extremely boring and tedious. It got to the point where the boredom turned to resentment, and I would eventually end up crawling up on the crate, standing on the crate, sitting on the crate, and even pissing on the corner of the crate.

As for the other guy, he would just walk around by himself, and I would sneak off away from the post to have some smokes. I smoked like a chimney at that time. At least a pack and a half a day. So you can't smoke when you're on post because you're in the middle of the desert, and it's dark at night. You light up a cigarette and you're giving away your position if there is somebody out there watching you with night-vision goggles. You even light the cherry on the end of your cigarette, it'll illuminate your entire body on night-vision goggles. So I'd walk away from the post to go have a cigarette around some sand dunes that were nearby. I'd walk about a hundred meters out and crawl up on a dune where I could still look down and see the crate.

I did this same routine for the first two nights. I'd just smoke, check on the post, and then lay on the sand dude and stare up at the clear night skies. With no ambient light and a restricted airspace, there was nothing standing in the way of me and the most beautiful spectacle of the cosmos up there.

On the third night, the other guy decided to come out and have a cigarette at the same time I did. We both just sat there, smoking, not saying anything, and just stared at the stars.

I don't know why I did it, but I just decided that I wanted to look up at the stars with the night-vision goggles we were supplied with. They were the best the military had at that time. You could see millions upon millions of more stars than with your naked eye. So I put them on, and for about ten minutes, I just stared up in wonder, gazing at the stars, meteorites, and a few passing satellites. And then I saw something else. Something that would change everything.

As I was looking through the goggles, I saw this pinpoint of light that came from my six o'clock position, shot up to my top dead center, my 12 o'clock position, and then it made a ninety-degree left-hand turn and shot off to my nine o'clock position. It did not slow down once as it did this. It went from horizon to horizon in under two seconds!

And then it happened again. And again. It repeated every few seconds over the course of a minute or two. No decrease in speed. No arc to its turn. It maintained constant velocity. It traversed from horizon to horizon in less than two seconds. It made no discernible noise. Through the goggles, I couldn't tell if it had any color, as everything appears in shades of green, but it was brighter than the brightest star.

My best guess was that this light was about one hundred thousand feet up in altitude, which is basically skirting the edge of our atmosphere. This was not an airplane or a satellite, because again, we were in restricted flight areas. And I could discern satellites earlier in the night as I was watching the skies. Satellites don't move like that. The amount of thrust that it would take to make a satellite do a ninety-degree turn at that speed would be insane.

I took off the goggles and handed them to the other guy. He put them on and asked me, "What am I looking for?"

I told him, "You'll know when you see it."

I watched as he searched the sky with the goggles. I could tell he locked on something. He didn't say a word. Then I watched his head drop down and swing to the left. That was when I knew he'd seen it. And he'd seen it make the same exact motions I'd seen. That was when he took the goggles off, handed them back to me, and lit up a cigarette. He got up again, didn't say a word, and walked off.

I struggled with whether or not to alert anyone of what we'd seen. But then it dawned on me. I couldn't risk it. We had walked away from our area of responsibility to smoke, and it would have been disastrous for us to admit what we were doing when we saw what we saw. We never spoke about it again for the remainder of our time posted together. But that night stuck with me for many years to come.

I do believe that whatever it was I saw that night had a direct correlation to whatever it was in the crate we were guarding. Seeing all the people from the Department of Energy on the base was the first indicator. Given the fact that the Soviet empire had collapsed, and given the fact that at the time, it was a known issue to have lost or stolen nuclear devices from the Soviet Union, that was something people were looking for actively, and trying to account for nuclear weapons. We even had security briefings on this very thing. So initially, I thought maybe this was an exercise. Whatever was in the crate was ours, and it was probably something that would emit a radioactive signature that our satellites or our sensor tech on our aircraft would be able to identify, in an effort to train our guys on how to look for lost or stolen nuclear devices. Because if you're doing an aerial survey, you're putting giant x's on the ground to zoom the cameras in on. So I assumed that maybe what was in this crate was something that would trigger the sensors on the aircraft that were looking for this. And I just left it at that for years. But then, after doing some more digging, I realized that my original theory was far from the possible truth.

While the incident occurred in 1995, it's now 2023, and I've had an inordinate amount of time to research, dig, investigate, and pull information that led me to a rather unsettling conclusion as to the content of the crate. Remember that when this event occurred, it had only been five years since the collapse of the Soviet Empire. Nearly overnight, portions of the former Soviet Union fractured and became their own nation-states. Commanding generals and officers of the former Soviet military went to bed one night as high-ranking officers of the Soviet empire. They woke up the next without a country, without any political allegiance to their new home, and without a means to provide for their family. But they had access to portions of the massive stockpile of nuclear weapons now residing in their new country, which could be sold on the international black market.

Operation Ellipse Foxtrot, based on my research, was a "routine" joint-forces military training "exercise"—and it appears it was used as cover for a real-world incident. All information now points to the assumption that US Special Forces, in conjunction with Jordanian forces, intercepted a shipment bound for Iraq. It is widely known that in 1995, more than eight hundred sophisticated gyroscopes for intercontinental ballistic missiles were shipped from Russia to Iraq and intercepted by Jordanian authorities.

However, this was not the first such interception, and I strongly believe that earlier intercepts were of actual fissile material. While the gyroscopes had been removed from the command modules of Russian SS-N-18 submarine-launched ballistic missiles being destroyed under arms control treaties, I have evidence to support my claim that the contents of my crate were actual fissile material from a dismantled Soviet SS-24 nuclear warhead purchased illegally by Iraq and bound there for eventual use against the national security of the United States.

Further research has uncovered a trail that hints to the final dispensation of that crate and its contents, and I do not believe it was ever delivered to the United States or stayed under our control. My research points me to a trail that takes the crate to Cairo, Egypt, as a "gift" by the US government to the government of Egypt, a government now finally outside the sphere of influence of the Soviet empire and one looking for allies in the new world. What better deterrent would we have than to possess a Soviet nuclear weapon, placed in service in a non-NATO country we were courting for friendship, and if things in the Middle East got out of hand, that nuclear device could be used? The radiation signature would point directly to that of Russia and not us or our allies.

The connection between UFOs and nuclear material is well documented, and I assume that if what I saw in the Jordanian sky that night was indeed an off-world alien craft, it may have detected a nuclear signature in an area that never had those emissions previously, and it was surveilling the crate and its content.

The sighting event itself has had less of an impact on me than the trail of evidence that led me to believe the crate contained active warheads from an SS-24 and that the US government may have secreted the crate and the devices into Egypt for use in a plausible deniability scenario that could have started WWIII. The notion that, if this in the future proves to be an accurate assessment of the events, the United States was willing to possess a weapon of mass destruction, place it in operation inside the territory of a "frenemy," and develop first-strike capabilities within the European and African continents, which would point to Russia as the aggressor, gives me tremendous angst.

I am by no means an expert on geopolitics, international affairs, or military tactics; however I do feel I maintain a firm understanding of right and wrong, and if this scenario is accurate, then the United States government violated my trust.

That UFO event burned itself into my brain, and I think about it often. And my personal belief, after having seen what I saw and knowing what I know...

We are not alone.

THE FIRE FIGURE IN THE OUTBACK

My name is Daylan. I had what I believe to have been a UAP close encounter experience while serving in the Australian military in 2009. A bit about my background. I did fifteen years in the Australian defense forces. The first eleven years in the Navy as an electronics technician for weapons and radar. In the last four years, I was a military working dog handler with the military police. While posted with the military police, I was stationed at a remote base in the Australian Outback, not far from a town called Katherine, in the Northern Territory.

It was around the end of the dry season in September, and we were hosting international exercises with the Americans, as widely publicized every year. This year was no different. It was a weekend. I was on night shift, so would start about sunset, and I usually worked with one particular colleague and my police dog.

This night, we loaded up the truck and drove down to the flight line. Now in this particular place, the flight line is dispersed in bushland, which means that craft don't sit on a nice concrete pad all lined up in a row with spotlights on them. They're dispersed, in the dark, with around a five-kilometer radius. And in between each are unloading areas and taxiways.

To give an idea about Northern Australia, it's either hot and wet or hot and dry. This was in the hot and dry season, and the wildlife is quite thick. There's bats, kangaroos, snakes, spiders, and stuff you don't even recognize.

So we got out there just before sunset and unpacked everything. Then we started walking the perimeter, and I was chatting with my colleague. And he started telling me a story about how in September of the year before, he had been patrolling with another dog handler, and he'd had a UFO sighting.

So a little about me. I love astronomy, and I'm a science fiction nerd. So when he told me this, I was like, "Hell yeah! Tell me all about it!"

So he told me this story about three stars flying overhead, stopping on a dime, and then suddenly dispersing in a split second, in all different directions, and disappearing.

I was like, "Holy shit! That's amazing!"

But where we were and what we were doing, I started thinking that what he saw could have been anything. Katherine is one of the UFO hot spots of the world, especially at that time of year.

We started walking. The sun was starting to set. Now, this place usually has a lot of bats. A huge bat colony, and it's usually teeming with life. I mean, everything's alive, and everything's got something alive on it. But right now... there was nothing. I put it down to maybe the bats had moved on, because they were kind of troublesome and, at the time, interfering with the aircraft. There were usually a ton of kangaroos. But we'd recently had a kangaroo crawl, so I thought that the hunters had just erased a lot of them off the face of the Earth. I didn't think anything more of it.

So we were walking on the perimeter, laughing about this story. And then my dog suddenly stopped dead in his tracks. Admittedly, he wasn't the best police dog in the world. He was quite friendly, soft, distracted and quite uninterested in being a police dog. So he stopped on a dime, and he was looking at the horizon. And then he started growling. And my colleague started yelling, "Oh my God... look! There they are!"

I looked up, and there were three star-like objects flying towards us, in a sort of wide V formation. There were no flashing lights. Nothing like that. They were slowly flying, in perfect formation, and just stopped right there. The lights were about ten degrees apart, which is like when you look up and put your hand up, it's about a handspan and a forty-five-degree-angle line of sight.

So to my mate, I asked, "Is this what you're talking about?"

He told me, "Yeah. This is it. They're gonna just disappear in a minute. Watch!"

We were looking and looking, and nothing was happening. And then they just stopped there. And it was like this feeling... like they were looking at us. We were looking at them. And then my dog started barking. Which he never does, even when he's supposed to!

I was thinking, *My dog can see this...*

I then thought about radioing my boss, asking if we had any "unscheduled scheduled but not really scheduled" flying activity going on. And as I was calling him, the outer two objects just shot off in opposite directions. I'd never seen anything like this. I've been in the radar rooms. I've seen all sorts of weird crap. But nothing that flies this fast. And I was on a base with fighter jets... but whatever these things were... they were the fastest I've ever seen.

The middle object remained. We were looking at it, waiting for it to do something. Meanwhile I radioed my boss and asked again about any "unscheduled scheduled but not really scheduled" stuff, and he was like, "No. Leave me alone. Get on with your job."

The object just stayed there. My dog was going crazy. And then there was this smell. It usually smelled like wet trees or flowers. But this was an electrical smell. Kind of like when you opened up an old radar cabinet and all that waft of old people's home and old rusty metal comes flying out at you. That was what it smelled like. And I was thinking, *Where the hell is that smell coming from?* There was no wind. No animals. No sounds. Just this stench.

My dog was growling at this point. My colleague and I were just standing there, and I was getting jelly legs. Then, all of a sudden, there was this vibration that I could only feel in my sinus cavities, my forehead, my lips, and kind of a little bit in my chest. I thought my dog could pick it up, too, long before we did because he was going nuts. He was trying to bite off his leash. He was growling still, and his tail was between his legs. I was looking around, and there didn't seem to be anything out of the ordinary, so I tried to calm him down because we had to do this patrol.

So we were moving around the perimeter, and the sun was now below the horizon. This middle object was still stationary in the sky. In fact, it was geostationary. We figured this out because we watched the stars for over an hour move as they do, and this thing was still exactly where it had stopped.

We did an entire walk of the perimeter of the flight line, and this thing was still exactly where it stopped. Now it was slowly brightening and dimming. Meanwhile, the dog was jumping at everything and looking over his shoulder. We got out flashlights, and we were looking all around us for anything that could be making the dog act this way. Still nothing.

So as time passed, we went back to our truck, which was parked amongst one of the overlays. I put the dog in the truck to hopefully calm him down, which it did. My colleague and I were then lying on the tarmac, watching this object, which still remained stationary in the sky. There was still this weird smell and almost a humming noise happening around us.

After a few moments, my colleague went to go relieve himself in the bush. I was looking into the distance, and in the most heavily dense bush area, one of the corners of the area we were patrolling, I could see this glow. It was orange in color. Kind of like a fire. It was flickering like a fire. Scrub fires are not unusual at that time of year, especially in this area. So they do spontaneously happen, because under the base is an underwater river system and cave system, and the fires do burn. Don't ask me about the science of this, but it does happen. They sort of pop up every now and then. So I thought maybe it was something like that. Also, that metallic smell was getting heavier at this point.

My colleague made his way back, and I showed him the flickering glow and told him it might be a scrub fire. We immediately called the fire department, and they told us to have a look at it and see if it was a big one. If it wasn't, it should go out on its own. If it was a big one, splash some water on it.

So we started walking towards it to get a better look. I didn't want to take my dog out, but I did. And he was virtually skidding backwards as we were trying to walk forwards towards this light glow of orange. We got to about fifteen meters when my dog was crawling up the back of my pants. At that point, he was once again growling from between my legs.

The closer we got, the more I noticed details of the glow. It looked like a ball of flame. But no smoke. No smell of burning. Everything was misty in between. Kind of like someone had a smoke machine and just made this haze of a ball thing. It was about three meters wide and about the same height. And I could see something in it.

I squinted my eyes, and this is where it gets weird. It looked like there was a pair of legs in there. Not like standing in there burning, but the shape of legs in this light. There was no body attached to it. There were no feet. All I could see was a pair of skinny little calves, knees, and thighs. Everything else above was obscured by this orange flaming glow.

So at this point, I told my colleague, "We've got an intruder!"

We called the fire department again, and they came out and actually saw it. They could see the light we were talking about.

They came rushing towards it in their truck, and just as they arrived, the light blinked out. Like someone turned off a switch.

We were still, like, fifteen meters away, and the driver asked, "What the hell is that!?" I told him that we didn't know but that they should get a closer look. So they took their truck towards it. We were walking behind the truck very slowly. I was dragging the dog with me as my colleague and I saw the fire truck shine a spotlight in front of them. They got to the corner where this bushland is. You can't actually access that place. You're almost standing at the edge of the taxiway and looking into it. And that was when we all saw something.

About ten meters in, we saw this empty patch. This oval-shaped empty patch of gray ash and sand. There was no vegetation. No footprints. There was absolutely nothing. But it was heavily bushed. And there were trees and stuff overhanging it. And they were untouched. There were no scorch marks. No smoke. No heat. Nothing to suggest that there had been a bushfire.

One of the firies said, "This is weird..."

So we were all standing there mystified, and the firies started to spray water on the patch of ash and sand. Because that solves everything, right?

Then they said, "Call us if it starts up again." And then they got in their truck and drove away, leaving myself, my colleague, and my dog standing there. And we took off as fast as we could back to our truck.

Meanwhile, this thing was still flashing above us! Which, in the excitement, we didn't even mention it to the fire department. I put my dog in the enclosure in the back of the truck, locked it up, and we were just standing there looking at this pulsing whatever. I was looking in the distance for this glowing orange fire thing again, fearing that ET or something was going to come tap me on the shoulder or something! Also, the humming and the smell were both still there.

It was about 4 a.m. at this point. The dog was exhausted, sleeping in the back, finally calm. So we were driving, and I was thinking to myself, *Do I report this?*

I ended up deciding not to because everyone knows I'm a bit kooky, and I was also the only female in the section at the time, and it was hard enough. I just didn't need extra problems.

So a little later, we did a drive-by again, and this thing was still in the sky! As I was looking up at it, it seemed to be getting smaller. I told my colleague, and we both watched it, waiting for something dramatic to happen. Instead, it just slowly rose and disappeared into the sky. As soon as that happened, the humming and the smell slowly dissipated over the course of the next hour.

At about 5 a.m., I had to get back to the section to do a handover, and I really didn't even know if I wanted to go back to the city. I wanted to get the hell out of there, but I wanted to stick around, too. I didn't want to leave the place. I wanted to see if something else happened. But it didn't.

Sunrise is usually when the kangaroos come out again and the bats do their big thing. But there was nothing. No birds either. It was a void, and it was only when we got back to the section that we started seeing the usual wildlife on the base.

I did end up speaking to my commander at the shift changeover the next day about what had happened. He quickly ordered me to have a drug test. He told me that it was obviously a scrub fire. And that something probably hit something metal underground, and that was what the smell was. And the rest of it... he believed we were just making it up. We were told not to write anything in a report about it.

Since that night, I've never been able to talk about it, really. I just talk about it with that same colleague, whom I remained friends with afterwards.

I live in Germany now, and I work with military radar systems once more. I do seek out other UFO stories from time to time, but I still haven't heard any stories remotely similar to what I saw and experienced.

I sometimes dream about those lights in the sky over the base. And I also dream about the legs in the fiery glow.

It was truly a night I will never forget.

SHADOWS OF WHITEMAN AIR FORCE BASE

My name is Adrian Reister. I had several unexplainable incidents occur while I was stationed at Whiteman Air Force Base in Missouri, between 2003 and 2007.

I joined the Air Force pretty much right out of high school. I had actually originally gone in to EOD (explosive ordnance disposal), which is essentially the bomb squad of the military. It was a very intensive and very difficult course. Unfortunately, I washed out of that course, and it was just one of those things. So after that, I was kind of what they call a student out of training for about a month or two, and then that was when they decided they were going to throw me on nuclear weapons. Basically, "You can't work on regular bombs, but we're gonna have you work on these nuclear ones over here." Makes sense.

So I didn't really have any other choice but to accept. It was a fairly interesting career field. There's a lot of secret stuff. So for my first year or so, I was basically on guard duty for the secured facilities. And the area where I worked was right next to the flight line. So I was able to see B2s, F-17s and A-10s take off and land a lot. I got pretty familiar with how these highly advanced aircraft maneuvered and functioned in the air.

The first event that happened to me was in 2005 while a transport of weapons was occurring. I can't say what day and time it was only because those transports are highly classified and could still be happening on the same days and times. But suffice to say, it was dark enough for me to see that there were stars and stuff in the sky.

We were in the middle of a maintenance cycle, and they needed an armed guard while they transported a weapon. That was me. As the transport team radioed to me that they were now transporting the weapon, I saw that there was this... orb, for lack of a better definition, bobbing above the tree line in the distance. At first I thought it was a star or maybe even a satellite, but it had this yellow and white tint to it and was much larger than the other stars in the sky.

So the weapon was still being transported down, and I was still kind of looking around, surveilling, and as the transport team pulled up with the weapon, this orb shot up, real quick, above the tree line. It kind of bobbed there for a little bit. The transport team was moving forward and backing the weapon into the facility, and then once they had secured the weapon inside the building, this orb just darted off to the north at a ninety-degree angle into the distance, and it was gone.

Later that year, I would have a similar sighting of the same orb-like phenomenon on the base while a group of contractors were working in the weapons storage area in what we call a "free zone," where they wouldn't need classified security clearances. My job that day was to watch after these contractors. But I did see this orb again, and it just hung there for a while, pulsating, and then it once again disappeared off into the distance.

Aside from these UFO sightings, there is one bizarre incident on base that haunts me until this day. This was in the spring of 2006. We were out on a maintenance cycle, so there wasn't any maintenance being done. Typically whenever we're not doing any maintenance, we're training crews. The more people we had, the easier it was for everybody else. But because they were training, they still didn't have clearance for certain areas. So we'd have to lock up the building. We'd pin it. So basically, there's these pins on the top and the bottom of the doors. If those specific doors haven't been opened, they should still have this tamperproof seal. Those tamperproof seals are a big thing on base.

So on this day, I was in the weapons support area because I had just transitioned from doing the nuclear operations side to doing weapons support. The training crews were in a separate bay in the back, working on a training bomb. I was essentially issuing toolboxes, chemicals, and helping issue anything they needed for their training. As they were locked away, I was on the computer doing my own thing.

As I was sitting there on the computer, I heard what sounded like water dropping on the floor. Or maybe footsteps. Which was a possibility. We had an eye wash station, and we had those emergency showers in the facility.

So I turned around and looked up. I was trying to see if there was anything there. There wasn't. I thought maybe I was hearing things. So I went back to doing whatever it was I was doing. And maybe a minute or two passed, and I started hearing those sounds again. This time, a bit louder. It distinctly sounded like bare feet on the painted cement floor. This time, I just whirled around, and I stood up, and I looked past the service counter.

All I could see was just this... shape. Of a person. It was standing about six feet tall. It was blurry and didn't reflect any light. If you've seen that dye that pretty much absorbs all light, it was essentially like that. I was just about to approach this shape when it quickly turned the corner into the administration area. So I started booking it and chasing this thing like a madman.

When I got in there, I didn't see or hear anything. But it was now my obligation to go around and look for this thing. And as I was going through, I didn't see anything. I was looking underneath chairs and tables. I looked in several of the offices and a conference room. There were really not a lot of places for this thing to hide. And in order for it to have left the actual building, the only way was through the front door. It was an airlock-system-style door, and you essentially had to go through one set of doors into an antechamber, and then from the antechamber, somebody had to actually let you in and out of the building. Basically... you're going to notice when someone leaves the building. And I heard nothing. I looked around a bit more, but found nothing. But even more interesting, none of the seals on any of the doors had been broken.

So what the hell had I just seen? As far as I knew, it was a ghost. Even if I had thought it was some kind of infiltration of some sort, I didn't have any physical evidence on me that there was somebody there. There were no sensors being tripped. There was no video evidence. There was essentially just me saying, "Hey, I think I saw something running down the hallway." And I wasn't about to report it either because I was afraid of the ridicule I might face. Even worse, I was afraid I'd have to take a psych evaluation or that I could even lose my security clearance. So I remained silent about it. Some people may think that if this was an intrusion on the base, that I definitely should have reported it. But you have to know that I was only nineteen years old at the time. I wasn't about to risk my job.

I don't know what those orbs were over the base. And I don't know what the shadow figure was. But it happened. All of it. And looking back, I wish I could have told someone. But there was no reporting mechanism back then. And the public wants more transparency by the military and government on UFOs. And all these people who have had experiences, there hasn't been anything to make them feel comfortable enough to come out and say anything. So if it's through me doing this, I hope I can make a wide enough path for them to follow through.

I'm all for UFO transparency. We deserve the truth. I hope we'll get there someday. Things have certainly picked up pace within the last few years.

I'm confident that within the next five to ten years, we'll see something change. Something big.

MISSING TIME AT NOVEMBER 5

My name is Mario Woods. I'm sixty-seven years old, and I live in Brunswick, Georgia. I currently work for a paper company called Georgia Pacific. I served in the United States Air Force from 1975 to 1983, in Security Police. In 1977, I had a UFO encounter at a nuclear missile site at Ellsworth Air Force Base.

After Air Base Ground Defense training, the first base that I was stationed at was Ellsworth. I was eighteen at the time, and all of a sudden, I was in a missile complex in the middle of nowhere in South Dakota. It was very eye-opening. At the time, I didn't really comprehend the scope of the global threat in terms of the Cold War. Then all of a sudden, I was thrust into the middle of it. There were times when I actually got to go down inside a silo and put my hands on a missile. It was both unsettling and also exhilarating.

Our base had approximately 150 missiles, which included ICBMs. As a security police officer, we live on these launch control facilities for three days at a time. There were six security police officers. Four of which were response personnel, two were flight security controllers, one was a facility manager, and then there was a cook. Then there were two other officers who were underground at all times, manning the launch control capsule.

So on this particular night, my partner was a man named Michael Johnson. He was working vacation relief for my normal partner, and being that he outranked me, he was a team leader. We were at November 1, a different site from where this event would eventually take place. So around 9:20 p.m., I stepped outside to the parking lot to smoke a cigarette and to stretch my legs. It was freezing. Had to be about 12 degrees Fahrenheit (approximately -11 Celsius). And that was when I saw an object at about a thirty-degree elevation in the sky.

I was kind of confused by it, because it was so large, and it was so bright. But it was a different intensity of light that I'd never seen before. At first, I thought it was two B-52 bombers, as we did support a strategic bomber squadron at Ellsworth Air Force Base. Sometimes, they'd fly these things for training. And they'd fly them really low, like four hundred feet off the ground. And they had some really big lights on them. So I thought maybe they were in tandem behind each other or something. It was so strange that it kept my attention, especially since I couldn't tell if it was moving towards us or if it was stationary. But I'd say it was about seven or eight miles away and was about the size of a quarter of the moon's diameter.

It was up there for such a long time. And that was when I remembered something my father had taught me from his time in the US Navy. Sometimes, they'd flash their ship's lights at other ships for communication. So I decided to go inside, and I walked up to the panel there. And it was just a one-switch control. Twelve to fourteen lights around the facility that illuminated the perimeter and the building. So I flipped the switch off. No sequence or SOS or anything like that. Just sort of for fun.

And then I went back outside and looked up at that thing in the sky. And whatever it was, all of its lights also flipped off, then on, then off again. I kind of just laughed to myself and thought, *Well, that's interesting!*

That was when I thought maybe it was helicopters. Sometimes helicopters did trips out to our sites, either dropping off people or bringing maintenance teams out or something. So I headed back inside again, excited this time, and I told Michael that he had to come check it out. But he was glued to the TV. So I repeated this process of turning the lights on and off and going outside and checking on this object. Sure enough, it flipped its lights on and off two more times, making it three in total before I could no longer see the lights. That was when I thought to myself, *Well, the show's over.* Little did I know, the show was just beginning.

At approximately 12:30 a.m., the Launch Control Center phone went off in the flight security controller's office. This is a direct line between the flight security controller and the missile combat group down below. We got called out for various reasons on occasion, such as when birds or something would fly through the antenna array. But this was different. This was an outer and inner zone alarm at November 5, where the missile silo was. In other words, this was something serious.

We got our briefing, gathered our gear and weapons, and loaded up into our pickup truck and started to make the twelve-minute trek from November 1 to November 5. Michael was driving. We got to Highway 79, and I looked over to my right, and there was this really strange glow, miles away, in the direction of November 5. I said to Michael, "Dude, that's that object sitting on November 5!" And all he said to me was, "Whatever, man."

We continued our journey to November 5, and when we got closer, that was when I saw it. This... object. It was directly above the site, about ten feet in elevation. And it completely dwarfed the site. It was a round sphere. It had no hard edges, no protrusions, no engines, and no visible signs of propulsion. The exterior didn't even look solid so much as it almost looked gaseous. It just hovered there, completely silent.

This object was so large that I couldn't even see the top of it from the windshield of the truck. I was about to say something to Michael, and when I looked over at him, he was bathed in some kind of bluish-white glow. He was stuck to the steering wheel, too, not moving at all. I was yelling his name, and he was just... frozen there, staring up at the thing. While I was looking up at it, the atmosphere in the truck got really thick. Like a pressure inside the truck. And I could almost smell the air. Like it was electrified somehow. I could barely breathe. It was as if the interior of the truck was being vacuumed out.

This was when I rolled down my passenger-side window, and I pulled up on the windowsill using the side mirror. That was when I took my Maglite out, and I flashed it at this thing, just like before. No sequence. Just trying to get its attention. And I watched. Nothing happened. So I slithered back down into my seat, with my M16 between my legs, and put my head down. I told Michael, "It'll be okay." I was trying to reassure him. But also, I was trying to reassure myself. "It'll be okay," I kept repeating. That was the moment when that pressure released in the truck, and I could start breathing again.

As I caught my breath, I could sense something to my right outside the window. And before I could even look, this rush of both tunnel vision and fear came over me. I turned to roll the window up, and then was when I saw something outside the window. There were these... figures. Bathed in shadow. All of a sudden, my eyes became very heavy, and I blacked out.

The next thing I remember, I opened my eyes, and it was complete darkness. I was trying to gather myself, and I could faintly see Michael still frozen to the steering wheel, not moving or talking. I yelled his name, but he didn't react at all. I reached down, and I popped the door open. I activated my Maglite as I stepped out of the truck. The first thing I noticed was that my boots sank directly into the ground. It was pure mud. This was odd because we had been on pavement when we'd stopped the truck in front of November 5.

My eyes were beginning to focus more at this point. I looked ahead of me, and there was this tall, white wall. I was very confused by this. My eyes followed it from left to right, and it went on and on as far as I could see. And the only thing I could think to myself was, *Where the hell is November 5?*

That was when the radio crackled to life. I could hear someone on the other end.

"Wing Security Control to November 1. What's your location?"

I expected Michael to answer it, but he still wasn't responding to me.

"Wing Security Control to November 1. Come in."

They repeated this several times over the radio as I continued waiting for Michael to respond. But he didn't. So I got back in the truck, and I started shaking him. I tried moving him, getting him to answer the radio. He wasn't budging. Just stuck to that steering wheel, still staring straight ahead. It was as if he was in some sort of catatonic state.

I responded to the WSC call. They asked what my location was, and I didn't know what to tell them.

"Sir, this is Senior Airmen Woods. I don't know where I am. All I see is a white wall."

There was silence for a moment. They responded by ordering me to perform one-minute security checks with them until they could triangulate our location. This was a first for me.

As I waited, I noticed that it was now getting light outside, which made absolutely no sense. We had left November 5 around 12:30 a.m. Again, confused, I looked down at my watch. It was functioning just fine. But the time made no sense to me. Sure enough, as it started to get brighter outside, my watch read almost 6:30 a.m. Over five hours had somehow passed.

About twenty minutes passed while I continued doing the

security checks. At that point, a total of three backup alert teams arrived in three different vehicles. They parked about twenty yards away from us. Out of one of the vehicles came a Sergeant Garza. He approached our truck, and I stepped out. He ordered me to stay in the truck. At this point, I almost felt like I had done something wrong. In fact, I started realizing, we hadn't performed our security check on November 5. My job was to do an internal patrol around the inside of the fence. We hadn't done that.

"What happened?" I asked Garza.

His response was blunt. "I can't talk about it."

I pressed him again, asking if anyone had secured November 5.

"I can't talk about it. We're here to bring you back to November 1 Control."

I did as I was told, and we were able to get Michael into the passenger seat. He was clearly still very shaken up and refused to speak. I took over driving and followed the response teams back to November 1.

As I was driving, I continued to look at the surroundings. And it finally hit me. We were on the back side of the Newell Lake Dam. That massive, white wall was part of the dam. The problem with that was that it was approximately six to seven miles from November 5. As I was driving, I was thinking to myself: *How in the world did we get seven miles away from November 5 without me remembering anything?*

Next thing I knew, we were at the Launch Control Facility. The first thing they did was separate Michael Johnson and me. They brought him to a back room. I assume they were trying to assist him medically for whatever was going on with him, as he was still nonresponsive.

So I sat down and answered questions from my flight chief for probably half an hour. I just told him everything that I had seen and what I had experienced. His most pointed question for me, however, was simple: "Do you know how you got to where you were?"

I told him, "No, sir."

The questions just kept coming. I told them everything I remembered from the first time I saw the object at November 1 and when I blacked out. He kept pressing me. At this point, I just felt in disarray and felt almost panicked. I asked if I could go to the restroom, which they allowed me to do.

I went into one of the stalls in the restroom and sat down on top of the toilet. I just held my head in my hands, trying to gather myself. All of a sudden, I felt as if I were leaving my body. I thought I was dying. The feeling went from the top of my head, down through my stomach, and out of my feet. To this day, I've never heard of anything like that. Whatever this was stopped almost immediately when I opened my eyes, and I could see these four furry feet walking by the stall door. It was a German shepherd drug dog. Turned out it was one of the law enforcement officers at Ellsworth. He actually had come in to check on me. I told him I didn't even know if I was okay or not. But the one thing I knew was that I was glad he came in there, because I had no idea what would have happened next in there if he hadn't come in. I honestly felt like I was leaving my body.

They probably kept me there for another hour or so until another response team came out to replace Michael Johnson and me. Soon after that, I was brought back to Ellsworth Base and to the Security Operations building. I was ushered directly to my squadron commander's office. In the room were also the base commander, my flight chief, a nurse, a man in a suit, and members of the Office of Special Investigations. I once again briefed them on what I remembered happening. To this day, I have no idea who the man in the suit was who was in the room with us.

While there, I had to write out a preliminary report on what I remembered, and then I was brought to the flight surgeon's office, and I was examined for almost two hours. They checked on my normal vitals. Checked my eyes, nose, and throat. And then the flight surgeon said he had to take a few skin samples from me. This sort of caught me by surprise, and I asked him why he would need skin samples. He told me, "Well, your face and hand are burned on your right side." Sure enough, I looked at my hand; it looked like I'd been sunburned. Again, I had no idea what to make of this, other than it must have been from the object we'd seen hovering over November 5.

The flight surgeon took two of the skin samples, put them in two separate vials, and then they released me to go back to my squad commander's office. When I got there, there were a few more moments of me debriefing him, and then it came. "You cannot, under any circumstances, discuss this with anybody."

And with that, I was dismissed of my duties for the night and went home. As I was attempting to come to grips with this incident, I began to have strange dreams of that night. Every single time, in the dream, when something was about to truly show itself, I'd get this overwhelming sense of dread. And every time, I'd wake up in a pool of sweat.

Two weeks later, I was in my apartment in Rapid City. There was a knock on my door. When I opened it, I was surprised to see Michael Johnson standing there.

"Michael! Man, it's good to see you!" Mind you, I hadn't seen him since they'd ushered him off to that separate room after the incident.

All he said was, "What do you remember?" So he came in and sat down, and we started exchanging our recollections. We even drew the object over November 5, and our drawings were strikingly similar.

I asked him what had happened to him when we were in the truck, and he told me, "I don't know what happened. Whatever it was, it just took me over." I also asked him if he could hear me yelling his name and shaking him. He said, "No. I didn't hear you. But I did hear something..."

I asked him what that something was. And I'll never forget

his answer. "I heard many other voices telling me not to be afraid. But... I wasn't in the truck when I heard these voices. I was lying down somewhere." Then he said something that shook me to the core. "I saw your mittens on the ground where I was lying down." This led me to believe that wherever he was lying down, I was there with him, and we were no longer in the vehicle.

The last thing Michael Johnson said to me was, "I was scared to death."

I thanked him for coming to talk to me. I assumed we'd see each other again on base and talk more about it. I wanted to piece this puzzle together. Little did I know, that would be the last time I would ever see Michael Johnson. He was soon moved to a different base, and we never spoke again.

After a few weeks, I was removed from November Control and reassigned to Kilo Control near Sturgis, South Dakota. It became abundantly clear to me that the powers that be did not want Michael Johnson or me speaking to one another any longer about what had happened that night.

Later that year, I would go to a movie theater to see the new Steven Spielberg film at the time, *Close Encounters of the Third Kind*. I remember distinctly the scene at the mailbox when Richard Dreyfuss' character, Roy Neary, looks out his parked truck's window and sees a rack of mailboxes violently shaking. A moment later, a UFO that had been hovering over him directs a beam of light onto his vehicle. That scene freaked me out so badly that I had to get up and leave the theater.

I struggled for so many years to make sense of whatever happened that night. But the biggest struggle was not knowing what happened in those five hours of missing time. So I sought to find answers any way I could.

In 2017, I arranged a hypnosis session with a trained hypnotherapist by the name of Bob Upson. These are excerpts from the transcription of my session. At this point, I'm recalling when I got back in the truck and looked out the window. Under hypnosis, I was sobbing as I started to relay what happened:

HYPNOSIS SESSION WITH MARIO WOODS: CONDUCTED BY BOB UPSON ON OCTOBER 5, 2017

Upson: What's Michael doing?

Woods: He's just sitting there, looking straight forward.

Upson: What happened next?

Woods: I notice shadows on my right, on the other side of the road, moving toward the vehicle. They're beings. Four of them. And one taller one. It has a bald head and a long face. He looked through me.

Upson: What are the small figures doing?

Woods: One of the small beings reached in and touched my arm, my shoulder. It was like an electrical shock. But I can breathe easier; as soon as he touched me I can breathe easier. There was another craft, another craft... it's not as big, but there's another craft; it's blue-silver. It's pulsating from the top of it, like rings of light shooting up in the air, like energy or something. But it's sitting on the ground. The door of the truck opens; I didn't open it... but I'm moving away from the truck, floating, toward the smaller craft. Then, I don't know, everything just went black.

Upson: Where's Michael?

Woods: I don't know... I was moved away from the truck. I think I'm lying down.

Upson: What are you lying on?

Woods: I don't know. Nothing I can feel or sense; nothing that I can see.

Upson: What's around you?

Woods: I don't know. A void; there's space around me, like I'm in the middle of nowhere. It bothers me, but it doesn't bother me... I feel wet. Warm, wet.

Upson: Do you have clothes on?

Woods: I don't know. I don't know where I am, but I don't have my weapon. I see the four small beings approach me. They're all around me. I'm being told that I'm going to be looked at.

Upson: What does that mean to you?

Woods: I'm going to be examined; something's wrong with me.

Upson: Who's telling you that?

Woods: The one that's closest to my head. His eyes are really big. But he said something—not to fear... I'm breathing something; it relaxes me... I see glimpses of light; it's lighter now. Not as dark. I'm in a room, some kind of room. Is it some kind of inspection area? I'm lying on a table. I don't have any clothes on. I feel something on me; do they have their hands on me? On my neck, on my lower back, on my right hip. They're moving my head. They move me on my side. I feel a pinch on my lower left side. On my left hip, like somebody's got a hold of me or something. I'm breathing this gas or fluid or something. I felt fear at first, but it's okay now.

Upson: Are they giving you any messages?

Woods: No, they're just telling me not to fear. Then I ask, "Where's Michael?" They tell me not to worry about that. My right hand is hurting now; it's hurting a lot. A lot of pressure in my wrist.

Upson: Do you know what's causing it?

Woods: I can't see it. But whatever it is, it's not good. There's one being to my left; he puts his hand on my chest. Its left hand; it has left and right hands just like we do. Two legs. Small stature but their grip is strong... he leans down close to me and looks right down in me; way down in me. He tells me, "You'll remember what happened to you." They never moved their mouths; they talk to you inside. They talk to you via a gel, something they put inside you. It resonates. I ask, "How much longer?" They don't answer me.

Upson: What happens next?

Woods: I'm getting a bad chill; I'm getting a real bad chill. It's like they're taking the warmth away. I see this light above me; it's like a surgical light in an operating room. Now I see that big, tall bastard. He's back. He's standing by my feet and looking at me. I don't like this guy. The four little guys moved away from me. I don't like this!

Upson: Does the tall guy communicate with you?

Woods: No. He just stares at me. He just looks through me.

Upson: Does he look like the little ones, just taller?

Woods: No, his eyes are a different shape. His nose... is a lot thinner and longer. His forehead is higher. He has a uniform on... like a ranking officer or something. The little guys are not dressed like he is. They have a helmet or something. Their heads are not fully exposed; they're covered. They have this close-fitting attire, blue-silver.

Upson: Any markings on it or emblems?

Woods: There's three buttons, upper left collar... the arms are so long. How do you get arms so long?

Upson: Do they have fingers?

Woods: Yes, three fingers and one thumb. And they're long also; eight inches, eight or nine inches long. The middle finger is very long. But the little guys are different from the tall guy; he's really not a good person. He said something to them.

Upson: You heard it?

Woods: I heard it. Kind of a vibration, not a word. They're moving me... I can't see where I'm going, but I'm trying to. The only thing I'm feeling is what I'm breathing; I'm still breathing the gas or fluid. I think they're putting me to sleep. They wanted me to rest.

Upson: So what happens next?

Woods: I'm in darkness. I'm just completely left alone. I'm afraid that nobody is with me.

Upson: What do you hear?

Woods: I don't hear nothing. It's scary; I don't hear nothing or feel nothing. I just feel like my mind is floating all alone. I feel disconnected from my body. I feel like my consciousness could go anywhere, like I could go to the Moon. It's kind of scary... I don't know what this is.

Upson: What happens next?

Woods: I don't know what happens next.

Upson: When is the next time you see Michael?

Woods: In the vehicle. I open my eyes, and I'm back in the truck. I turn to my left and see him sitting there with his hands on the steering wheel. And I look around to kind of gather myself. What just happened? I hear the radio.

Upson: Who's on the radio?

Woods: It's Wing Security Control. They're saying our call sign. "November 1?" It's crackling; it's not a clear transmission. And I say, "Hey, Michael, are you going to get that? What the hell just happened?!" He wouldn't answer me.

To this day, I can't watch the hypnosis session that was recorded. And I still am wrestling with what happened. It's been forty-four years now, and it never goes away. As clear today as it was then.

In all my journeys, I never believed in hypnosis. But during my session, I experienced fear, pain and shock, as to the interaction of the once muddled beings I saw out the window right before blacking out. There were four. Three of them were about four feet tall, and the leader, in the rear, was about six feet tall. His face and body structure was different from the others.

That hypnosis session upset me so much that reliving the interaction with these beings actually put me into atrial fibrillation (AFIB). I was medically treated a week later with a cardioversion to restore my regular heart rhythm.

I don't know why this happened. But a part of me thinks that whatever happened, they didn't contact me. I contacted them. And they followed up on that. They knew that missile site was there, and it was connected to that launch control facility. I thoroughly believe that. So they went out there and set it off and knew I had to respond to it.

More recently, I was asked to meet with the staff of the Department of Defense's newly established All-domain Anomaly Resolution Office (AARO), to give my testimony about this incident. I very much look forward to giving my testimony, and maybe even finding some answers to what happened that night over November 5.

ABOUT THE AUTHOR

Ryan Sprague is the creator and host of the *Somewhere in the Skies* podcast, which has hit #1 on Apple Podcasts and was awarded Best UFO podcast in 2021 and 2022 in the Paranormality Podcast Awards. He is a TV series regular on *Ancient Aliens* and a lead investigator and co-host of the hit CW series *Mysteries Decoded*. He is the author of the best-selling book *Somewhere in the Skies: A Human Approach to the UFO Phenomenon*, which was recently implemented into required reading for college courses at Webster University and Mercyhurst University. Sprague also writes for the science and defense news site *The Debrief*. Speaking on UFOs, he has been interviewed on ABC News and 7News Australia. He has been featured in *Vice*, *Newsweek*, and the *New York Post*, as well as in various documentaries. He has consulted for Amblin Entertainment, Entertainment One, and Discovery Plus. Born and raised in New York, he currently resides in Scotland and is a proud member of UAPmediaUK.

If you've had a UFO sighting or encounter experience
that you'd like to share on the Somewhere in the Skies *podcast,*
contact Ryan at: ***Ryan.Sprague51@gmail.com***

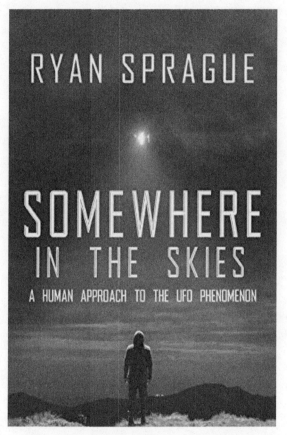

Somewhere in the Skies: A Human Approach to the
UFO Phenomenon

Made in United States
North Haven, CT
14 May 2023

36576830R00161